THINKING IT OUT

THINKING IT OUT
Christianity in Thin Slices

Ian Dunlop

Foreword by the Archbishop of York

Illustrated by Bruce Freeman

BRIDGE
PUBLICATIONS

PENISTONE · ENGLAND

Bridge Publications
2 Bridge Street, Penistone
Sheffield S30 6AJ

BR
96
.D84
1986

British Library Cataloguing in Publication Data

Dunlop, Ian
    Thinking it out : Christianity in thin
    slices.
    1. Christianity——Philosophy
    I. Title
    201   BR100

    ISBN 0-947934-07-3
    ISBN 0-947934-06-5 Pbk

Printed and Bound in Great Britain
by Whitstable Litho Ltd., Whitstable, Kent

Contents

REFERENCES

Aldous Huxley	The Gates of Perception	19
Walter Hylton	The Scale of Perfection	32
William Temple	Nature, Man and God (1935)	39
Laurens van der Post	The Night of the New Moon (1970)	52
Bertrand Russell	Marriage and Morals (1929)	55
Rollo May	Love and Will (1969)	passim
Joseph Fletcher	Situation Ethics (1966)	64
Dorothy Sayers	The Mind of the Maker (1941)	68
Helen Roeder	Saints and their Attributes (1955)	73
Yves Congar	Priest and Layman (1967)	80
E. Yarnold & H. Chadwick	Truth & Authority (1977)	87
William Temple	Readings in St John's Gospel (1947)	99
A. & R. Hanson	Reasonable Belief (1981)	99
David van Daalen	Real Resurrection (1972)	101
C.S. Lewis	Letters to Malcolm (1964)	104
Evelyn Underhill	Worship (1936)	117
R.G. Collingwood	The Principles of Art (1937)	121
Dom Gregory Dix	The Shape of the Liturgy (1945)	124
William Temple	Christus Veritas (1939)	131

Foreword

By the Archbishop of York

Sixteen years of answering questions for readers of The Church Times have taught Canon Dunlop how to pack a lot of wisdom in a small space. There is nothing superficial about these brief essays. Apt quotation, good illustration, and a simple directness of style make them easy to read, and well worth pondering at greater length.

I am glad that this selection from the 800 or so he has written is now made available in permanent form to a wider readership.

John Ebor

Bishopthorpe, York
11th September 1986

ILLUSTRATIONS

The striking simplicity and modernity of Bruce Freeman's illustrations is intentional. They are designed to complement the author's thoughts, not to compete with them. Each picture relates specifically to the theme of the section that it heads. Taken together, they constitute a whole in which images and symbols interact, in obvious and sometimes more subtle ways, to stimulate thought about the Christian faith. The reader is included in each picture; it is left to his creative imagination to see the implications of the rest of it.

Introduction

In June, 1970, the Editor of the *Church Times*, Mr Bernard Palmer, asked me to start a new weekly column in which I would invite readers' questions and attempt to answer them. He chose the title: *Thinking it Out*.

I have, therefore, in the course of the last sixteen years, contributed some 800 articles. Readers have from time to time been kind enough to ask if I would produce a selection of these articles in the form of a book. A slim volume is easier to keep than a pile of newspaper cuttings. In producing this work I have resisted suggestions from a number of publishers that I should 'work it up into something consecutive'. There are plenty of such books on the market. They offer Christianity in large chunks. I offer Christianity in thin slices - a bedside book for those who prefer their reading to be little and often.

In making this selection I have tried to present as wide a spectrum as possible. This is in the hope that some will find it useful as a basis for discussion and for adult or teen-age confirmation groups.

The problems of making such a selection are, however, acute. Many of the articles were relevant to a situation which has lost interest today. Many of them refer to correspondence in the pages of the *Church Times* and would only make sense if that correspondence were reprinted.

Inevitably, in the course of the years, I have repeated myself in various ways. I recall the words of Dr Johnson: 'Sir, mankind needs more often to be reminded than instructed.' If a point is worth making once it is probably worth making more than once. I make no apology for the fact that some of the repetitions which have occurred are reflected in this selection.

I once received an angry letter - what I call a 'splutter letter' - challenging me 'to come out in the open and categorically state that they are all genuine questions.' I categorically state that they are *not*. I nowhere claim that they are. My invitation to readers to submit questions does not often produce fifty-two *different* questions a year. Some have to be set aside as issues too large to be dealt with in 400 words. Some are too trivial. I once had the question: 'Why do so few Anglicans observe St Monica's day?' I could only have answered it with the further question: 'How on earth could *I* know?'   I doubt if the Editor would have felt that that dealt adequately with the theme.

Two interesting facts have come to light in reviewing the field which I have covered in the last sixteen years. One is the rarity of questions about Jesus Christ in person. It has not been possible to include in this book a special section devoted to Him. The other is that the subject on which I have most often been asked to write is passing the Peace.

Finally I want to thank my readers for much help and encouragement, and I hope that this selection of my articles will further assist them in their understanding of the Christian faith.

IAN DUNLOP

The Close
Salisbury
1986

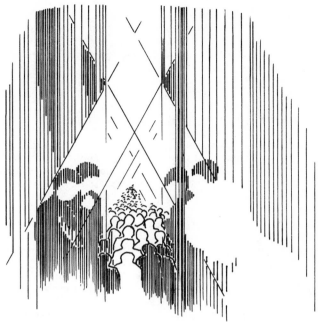

SECTION 1

Prayer

DAILY OFFERING TO GOD

'Although I want to pray, I often find that I can't.'

I WOULD have thought that, if you *really* wanted to pray, the battle was already as good as won. I suspect that the trouble with most people is more often that they *don't* pray than that they *can't*. I do, however, wish that the clergy would pay a lot more attention to this subject in their teaching. When did you last hear a sermon on prayer? When was there last some helpful advice on the subject in your parish magazine?

Archbishop Ramsey wrote in *The Charismatic Christ:* 'A terrible judgement rests upon the priest who is unable to give help or guidance because he has ceased to be a man of prayer himself.' Let us hope that your vicar does not fall within the Archbishop's strictures - but, if he does, why not use your need to awaken in him an awareness of his own? Some clergymen may have ceased to talk of prayer because no one has ever consulted them. It can be a great stimulus and encouragement to find that someone is really interested.

I am sure that the first important thing is to consecrate time - however short - *regularly* to prayer, even if nothing comes. There is a passive, receptive side to prayer which you might cultivate. Lord Tennyson once said: 'Prayer is like opening a sluice between the great ocean and our little channels.' More recently I have heard prayer compared with sun-bathing. I found that a useful comparison, and I pass it on.

A warning should be given to those who make excessive or exclusive use of the prayers of others and never develop their own praying. For someone in your position I would give the opposite advice. If nothing comes, why not see whether someone else's words cannot help you? Only remember that they are like crutches. The object is to learn to walk without them.

But I still cannot really believe that *nothing* ever comes to you! Have you *nothing* for which to express thankfulness? Have you *nothing* for which to express repentance? Have you *no* problems on which you need guidance?

There is a prayer by Dr Johnson which ends: 'Make me to remember, O God, that every day is thy gift, and ought to be used according to thy command. Grant me therefore so to repent of my negligence that I may obtain mercy of thee and pass the time which thou shalt yet allow me in diligent performance of thy commands.' At the very least you can offer every day to God in this sort of way.

HOW TO START PRAYING

'Why do so few of the Anglican clergy ever give instruction in prayer?'

THE ANSWER to this question is that I do not know and I could not possibly know. Neither could I arrive at the answer by thinking it out.

However, I would hazard the guess that those who give no instruction find a difficulty in doing so. They are not alone in their problem. Why, for instance, are so few people ever given instruction in conversation?

I remember once inviting a shy young man to a mixed party in my rooms at Oxford. He was unaccustomed to female society and at the foot of my staircase he stopped in anguish and asked, 'What shall I say?'

How does one give instruction in conversation? I can only say that, if you are interested in your fellow humans and not pre-occupied with the thought of yourself as a conversationalist, you will soon enough find yourself able to converse.

In the same way one could say that, if you are interested in God and not pre-occupied with the thought of yourself engaging in prayer, you will soon find that it comes. It may well be lack of practice rather than lack of instruction which is the root of the trouble.

But to return to my shy young friend, I did in fact try to help him into conversation with those frightening females by telling him something about each of them as I introduced them. 'She is training to be a nurse ... she lives in Dorset ... she is keen on music.' There you have several openings to conversation straight off. 'Nursing? Do tell me *all* about your matron'; 'Dorset? Do you know Tarrant Gunville?' and so forth. The more that you know about a person, the easier it becomes to enter into conversation with them.

It is worth considering also what are the commonest barriers to conversation. One of the most obvious is the result of one party having offended the other. You may have to put your relationship right first. Remove the barrier, and the conversation will flow.

I believe most of this to be true of our conversation with God. It is a useful preliminary to prayer to think a little about the known nature of God. You might notice how often the Prayer Book starts a prayer by reminding you of some aspect of God's nature, and then builds the petition upon it. 'Almighty God, who hatest nothing that thou hast made ...' Notice also how many acts of worship begin by putting our relationship right by an act of confession.

This can be done also in private prayer. Start with some thought of God: his mercy, for instance. Think about some Bible story which illustrates this thought: the man who owed ten thousand talents, perhaps. Then pass to your own need of God's mercy and to those who stand in need of yours. You will find that you have passed from thinking about God to praying to him.

WHAT NEED TO PETITION GOD?

*'If God knoweth what things we have need of before we ask',
why do we need to ask?'*

'I BLESS GOD,' wrote Jean-Jacques Rousseau, 'but I pray not. Why should I ask of him that he would change for me the course of things? - I, who ought to love, above all, the order established by his wisdom and maintained by his providence, shall I wish that order to be dissolved on my account?'

There is often a true humility in your position. But, if Rousseau has put your case accurately, then I think it can be answered. He talks of asking God to *change the order* of things. We must not start with the idea of God as a sort of 'Prime Mover' who set a machine in action and cannot reasonably be asked to interfere with its regular functioning.

It is not for nothing that we call God 'Father'. No father worth the name would be a prime mover of some unalterable course. Personal relationships do not work like that. Jesus used the metaphor of parenthood when he said: 'If ye, then, being evil, know how to give good things to your children, how much more shall your Father ... give good things to them that ask him?'

To them that ask. Your question is still unanswered, but I hope that we have removed one misunderstanding. We must be clear that we do not imagine that we can add to God's information about our needs or inspire him to an increase of good-will by our petitions.

The phrase which I think best answers your question comes from a very useful little book called *The Meaning of Prayer,* by H.E. Fosdick. He writes: 'You can open the way for God to do what he wants to do. Prayer cannot change God's purpose, but prayer can release it.'

I like that word 'release'. God has a great respect for human freedom. There are many things which he will not do until we freely accept them. By offering in prayer our willingness to do his will ('Thy will be done') we often create the only circumstances in which he will act.

There is a wonderful passage about God's respect for

freedom in Berdyaev's *Dostoevsky:* 'Truth nailed upon the
cross compels nobody, oppresses no one; it must be
accepted and confessed freely; its appeal is addressed to
free spirits. A divine truth, panoplied in power, triumphant
over the world and conquering men's souls, would not be
consonant with the freedom of man's spirit, and so the
mystery of Golgotha is the mystery of liberty. Every time
in history that man has tried to turn crucified truth into
coercive truth he has betrayed the fundamental principle of
Christ.'

GOD'S WILL AND FREEDOM

*'Clergymen keep telling me that the answer to prayer is
sometimes NO. They cannot understand that my problem is
that the answer is always NO, if indeed it is an answer at
all. If God made Nature's Laws, why should I expect him to
intervene and change them for me?'*

TO TAKE your last point first – it is a great mistake to
regard any action by God as a contravention of his own
laws. The idea that the universe is a pre-set machine which
God started off and which 'rolls impotently on as Thou and I'
simply does not fit my experience.

It cannot be too strongly emphasized that laws do not
inhibit freedom – they are the absolute prerequisite for it.
It is the very dependability of nature's laws that enables
man to use them for his own ends. We would never get an
aeroplane from here to New York if the functioning of the
various laws of aerodynamics were not invariable.

Because they are invariable we are free to use them. A
vast number of the events in everyday life are not caused
by the predestined and predictable grinding on of the
cosmic machine, but by human intervention – and this
intervention in no case changes the laws or overrides them.
If, therefore, human beings can – and constantly do – alter
the course of events by using nature's laws to serve our
purposes, there is no logical reason that I can see why God
should not *a fortiori* do the same.

This is, however, purely theoretical. You may well be
prepared to admit with me that God *could* be continually
altering the course of events to suit his purpose and still
object that the world does not look like one in which he is
thus active.

It is precisely here that the need for prayer comes in. If the world were perfectly ordered by God so that nothing ever occurred that was contrary to his will, there would be no room for petitionary prayer. There could be nothing to pray *for*. But it would be a puppet world. We would all be obeying God because we had no choice. And a puppet world would have no value. The value of love is that it is freely given. Love that is forced is not love at all.

This, I think, is why God has always respected human freedom – even to a degree which some of us find very difficult to accept. It is evident that in many things he will not override our right to choose the wrong path. Certain things, it seems, will only happen if man freely assents to their happening. And man freely offering his will to be attuned to the will of God is no bad definition of prayer – or of a certain sort of prayer.

Prayer is not an attempt to impose our will upon God's will, but an attempt to discover what God's will is and, by offering our free assent, providing the conditions required for God to bring his will about.

DIFFERENT SORTS OF PRAYER

'In your article on the answer to prayer you say that in a perfect world there would be nothing to pray for. Surely your idea of prayer is far too narrow?'

I APOLOGIZE for the misapprehension. I was trying to answer a question which concerned the special problems raised by petitionary prayer. I certainly did not wish to be taken as implying that no other sort of prayer was possible.

There is, of course, another purpose to prayer, in the wider sense of the word, which would remain valid even if there were nothing for which we required to intercede. Evelyn Underhill, in *The Golden Sequence,* anticipates that she will be criticized for her omission of any reference to fellowship and service – which, she says, 'are often regarded as the substance, instead of the symptoms, of a living Christianity.' The book, she claims, is about 'that essential life out of which real fellowship and service must proceed.'

That 'essential' life is the life of communion with God. With this I wholeheartedly agree. It does, all the same, surprise me how much emphasis the New Testament puts on petitionary prayer. All the clauses in the Lord's Prayer represent petitions of some sort, except for 'hallowed be thy name.'

I sometimes think that Christian mystics have given inadequate emphasis to this fact. Evelyn Underhill herself often uses the term 'utilitarian' of a form of prayer of which she obviously disapproves. She insists on the primacy of adoration, which is her recipe 'to defeat the ignoble tendency to make God useful to man, instead of man useful to God.'

For those who use the Lord's Prayer as a framework for extended prayer, 'hallowed be thy name' will provide an excellent entry into this important activity of adoration. It is highly significant to me that it comes right at the beginning. But, since we do live in an imperfect world and petition is therefore by no means redundant, it is a useful corrective to the tendency 'to make God useful to man' that we start our petitions with 'thy will be done.'

But adoration can be regarded not as the means to any end at all but as an end in itself – a primitive, natural response of the creature to his Creator. In the same book there is a story related by Osbert Sitwell of a traveller who witnessed an ape bowing to the moon. 'I had seen,' was his comment, 'the birth of religion.' Thus Evelyn Underhill insists on the primaeval roots of adoration. 'The world's altar stairs begin in the jungle.'

PRAYERS FROM THE HEART?

'I was horrified to hear you say ... that we ought not to use the collects in our private prayers. Surely Cranmer's prayers are the finest expression in the English language of our duty to God?'

IF I REMEMBER the occasion rightly I did not say that you ought not to use the collects in your private prayers, but that you ought not *only* to use them. This 'only' is important. There is a difficulty about using other people's words.

In Rostand's great play, *Cyrano de Bergerac,* the heroine Roxane is in love with a simple but handsome soldier named Christian. Cyrano, physically ugly but with a noble soul and great poetic talent, is also in love with

Roxane - but he knows that his cause is hopeless and agrees, while he and Christian are soldiers in the front line together, to write his love letters for him.

At the critical moment before the attack Roxane turns up, so moved by the letters that she avers to Christian that she now loves him for his soul and not for his physical beauty. Christian, however, has discovered Cyrano's love which has been poured into these letters. He cannot accept Cyrano's explanation: 'I have the gift of putting into words ... what you perhaps feel.' He realizes that it is really Cyrano whom Roxane now loves and makes the statement: *'Je veux être aimé moi-même ou pas de tout'* ('I want to be loved for myself or not at all').

There is perhaps no finer expression of human love in the English language than in Shakespeare's sonnets. Sometimes they do express, as no other men's words could possibly express, what a lover does feel.

Yet in these thoughts myself almost despising
Haply I think on thee - and then my state,
Like to the lark at break of day arising
From sullen earth, sings hymns at heaven's gate
For thy sweet love remembered such wealth brings
That then I scorn to change my state for Kings.

[Sonnets, 29]

There is no reason why a lover should not offer Shakespeare's words to his beloved as saying what he cannot say himself.

And yet I cannot imagine that his own clumsy, fumbling attempts to speak his love may not strike deeper in his loved one's heart just because they *are his*. Shakespeare himself made this point in the wooing of Princess Katharine by Henry V. 'I know no ways to mince it in love but directly to say I love you.'

So, if the collects put in words what you feel but could not so happily express, then use them in your prayers. But do not let them be your *only* prayers. God does not have to be wooed in perfect language. He must be better pleased with prayers, however inept and poorly put, that come straight from your heart.

DOERS AND HEARERS

'Don't you think we have seen too much activity among Christians and not enough waiting upon God?'

I WONDER how this would apply to St Paul. He was a fairly active Christian, but he was able to say of his efforts: 'not I but Christ.' God, in fact, usually operates through human agents.

It has long been the practice of the Church to see in Martha and Mary the prototypes of two mutually exclusive psychologies and to take the story as concerning Divine approval upon the contemplative life. But there is a time and a place for everything.

When our Lord was present in the house, the opportunity to hear his word was of first importance. But who knows what effect her willingness to listen may have had upon Mary? We are not told that she spent the rest of her life in contemplation. Her moment of listening may have galvanized her into an activity which put Martha to shame.

The point is, surely, that Martha's restless desire to be doing something must be taken as self-inspired. Had she listened with Mary, her activity might have taken another form and a different orientation. We do not have to choose between waiting on God (hearing his word) and being a doer and not just a hearer of that word. It is the person who obeys God's commandment, not just the person who listens, who can be said to love God.

But of course, if you don't listen, you cannot obey. Like Milton, 'I cannot praise a fugitive and cloistered virtue ... that never sallies out and sees her adversary, but slinks out of the race where that immortal garland is to be run for, not without dust and heat.'

Having said that, I would agree that for most people far more attention should be given to contemplation, meditation and seeking the will of God. We pay much lip-service to prayer. Many church committees begin their sessions with the mumbled recitation of a collect. I wonder how many really pray for God's guidance in their deliberations.

Five minutes is not a long time – but it would seem an eternity for those who want to get on with the job. They might, however, get on far more effectively, with the real job, if they did consecrate five minutes to waiting on God before they began.

ADVICE ON PRAYER

'Why do we hear so few sermons on prayer?'

STRICTLY SPEAKING, I cannot possibly answer your question. It is certainly a subject on which I would have hoped that there were frequent sermons.

There is always a particular difficulty in helping someone with prayer; and this is that the very operation tends to focus attention on 'me-saying-my-prayers' which is likely to be counter-productive straight off. I think it was for this reason that Evelyn Underhill once wrote:

'Do not entertain the notion that you ought to advance in your prayer. If you do, you will only find that you have put on the brake instead of the accelerator. All real progress in spiritual things comes gently, imperceptibly, and is the work of God. ... Think of the Infinite Goodness, not of your own state. Realize that the very capacity to pray at all is the free gift of the Divine Love, and be content with Saint François de Sales' favourite prayer, in which, all personal religion is summed up: "Yes, Father! Yes and always Yes!"'

I think that we can learn a lot from the parallel with conversation. Nothing is more disastrous than self-conscious interest in 'me-making-brilliant-conversation.' People who go about it in that way are usually crashing bores.

The first qualification for successful conversation is a genuine interest in the person you are talking to, not a desire to improve your own ability as a conversationalist. Of course, if you are frightened of the other person, or if there is some sort of resentfulness on either side, this can also block the channel. Remove the obstacles, and the conversation will flow.

Having said all that, I do not mean that you cannot be helped in the matter of prayer. Evelyn Underhill must have been a very great help to a very large number of people; and, if you can get hold of her books, she may well be able to help you. When did you last read a book on prayer?

But the general advice I would give is to fix your whole mind and thoughts on God. If you find this difficult, the Bible is there to help you. It is, after all, mostly about God and can stimulate your thoughts if they need it. But conscious effort to improve your own performance is, I believe, likely to end in failure.

WHEN PRAYER FAILS

*'The headline, "Why prayers failed to save David Watson" -
if we believe in a blessed after-life, are we not inconsistent
in being upset when such prayers fail?'*

TAKEN to its logical conclusion, your argument could imply
that the sooner we get out of this world the better. It
raises the whole question of the value of life on this earth.
If life has no value, as W.S. Gilbert wrote:

> *Man is well done with it;*
> *Soon as he's born*
> *He should all means essay*
> *To put the plague away.*

But, if life on this earth does have value - as every
Christian must believe - then it exists in a mysterious
interrelationship with life hereafter.

By 'mysterious' I mean that this is something which
ultimately eludes our human understanding. I have never
been able to see any rhyme or reason behind the 'success'
or 'failure' of prayers for the recovery of the sick.
Sometimes what seems to be a miracle occurs, and sometimes
there is no apparent change in the situation.

During the euthanasia debates it was clear that many
Christians believe that only God can judge which is the
appropriate moment for a human life to end. There are
many difficulties and objections to this view, but I have no
space to go into them here.

What must be true is that God created each individual
human life for a purpose, and that it is this purpose which
gives meaning and value to that life. To recognize this
purpose is, I think, inconsistent with the view that the
sooner we get to Heaven the better.

But, if a man may glorify God in his life, so also can he
glorify God in his death. Suffering accepted can produce an
impressive blend of nobility and humility.

There comes a moment when one must recognize that the
scene has changed; that it is no longer in life but in death
that one must glorify God. How that moment is identified -
except as a matter of individual intuition - I do not know.
But it does bring me round to the prayer at Gethsemane
which might well be appended to all prayers for the sick:
'not according to my will, but according to thine.'

PRAYERS FOR THE DEAD?

'I was really shaken recently to hear a priest say that he never prayed for the dead. It had never occurred to me not to.'

I WOULD be interested to know what you pray *for* when you pray for the dead.

No prayer, for the living or for the dead, can ever take the form of an attempt to persuade God to change his mind. Such prayer would be grossly presumptuous, claiming that your idea might be better than his. So can we rule out straight-away the idea that by praying for the dead, we can in any way obtain for them the mercy of God which he would not otherwise have bestowed?

If it 'never occurred to you not to,' I wonder how much you have read of Church history. The issue which triggered off the Reformation was the claim by the Catholic Church to be able to manipulate what happened to the soul of a dead person - and of course to make a charge for doing so. The implication is obvious: a man may so live as to deserve considerable punishment in Purgatory and yet, if rich enough, avoid or at least diminish that punishment. The moral sense of the Reformers was outraged - and rightly.

I think that it is necessary to have *some* belief in Purgatory (though not the 'Romish doctrine' ruled out by Article 22) in order to pray *for* the dead at all. If a man's eternal destiny is determined at the moment of his death, what is there to pray for? I can pray for those alive in this world because I know something of the conditions of their life. I know practically nothing of the conditions of life hereafter.

But prayer is not all intercession. I think that the baby which the Reformers threw out with their bathwater was the desire to give expression to the sense of continuing communion with those who have departed this life. Thanksgiving is the most obvious note to strike: it is often the source of continued inspiration. I have often heard the bereaved say, 'He/she would not have wanted me to ...', or words to that effect. It is this sense of continuing communion which I think needs to be fostered.

Liturgically, the Church of England has always fought shy of the topic. In Cranmer's first Prayer Book there were still vague commendings of the soul to the mercy of God. In

1552 these were omitted. In 1662 the dead again get a mention, but never in the form of explicit intercession on their behalf.

I can see no harm in the phrase from the ASB, 'We commend all those who have died to your unfailing love, that in them your will may be fulfilled.' Does that count as praying for the dead?

Love

GOD AND ONE'S NEIGHBOUR

'We seem to hear rather a lot from the pulpit today about loving our neighbour, and not much about loving God.'

IT IS NOT possible to make a clear distinction between the two. The overlap is considerable, and a proper treatment in the pulpit of the command to 'love thy neighbour' would show that, at its best, this is a valid form of loving God. The parable of the Sheep and the Goats would provide the most obvious text.

St Teresa, whom one might regard almost as a specialist in the love of God, made the surprising statement: 'We cannot know whether we love God, although there may be strong reasons for thinking so, but there can be no doubt about whether we love our neighbour or no.' She therefore gives the advice: 'Be sure that, in proportion as you advance in fraternal charity, you *are* increasing in your love of God.'

I think that people who are suspicious of too much emphasis on loving our neighbours are afraid that God may be being left increasingly out of the picture. But what is so surprising about the parable of the Sheep and the Goats is that God does not even require that, in loving our fellow-men, we should actually be conscious of thereby loving him.

It seems, therefore, that while a strong case can be made for love towards man being an acceptable form of love towards God, no case can be made for so-called love towards God in the absence of love towards man. Anyone who claims to do so is denounced by the New Testament as a liar and a hypocrite.

This is not to say that there is no place for love that is offered simply and directly to God, but we should take St Teresa seriously in remembering that this must advance *pari passu* with fraternal love.

I often think of the twin commandments as the two legs which a Christian is given for his spiritual progress. We are told to walk and not to hop. As a matter of practical advice it is often true that, if one foot seems to be stuck, it is time to put the other forward. It is sometimes very difficult to love man. Most of us have times of sympathy with the Victorian Sir Walter Raleigh:

> *I wish I loved the human race,*
> *I wish I loved its silly face ...*
> *And when I'm introduced to one*
> *I wish I thought* What Jolly Fun.

At these moments it is probably wise to concentrate on loving God. If you go about it the right way you will find your attitude to man changed. There are also times when our love for God seems to have dried up. A real advance in charity to our fellows can often bring a new warmth of devotion. The two commandments should always be taken together.

HUMANITY AS INDIVIDUALS

'I try to be Christian, but, when I read Raleigh's poem, I wish I loved the human race ...', I can only say 'Amen'.

I HAVE to admit that, when I see a rush-hour crowd of smelly, down-at-the-mouth, selfish-looking humanity pushing its way onto the 'buses or trains, I find it difficult to love the human race, and therefore difficult to believe that God can love it.

I am here, of course, guilty of reducing God to human level, even if allowing him to be a bit of a Superman. 'I find it very difficult, so God must find it *fairly* difficult,' is the gist of my reasoning.

I note, however, that my revulsion for the human race which is engendered on such occasions is revulsion against humanity in the mass (notice that I used the word 'it' at the end of the first paragraph). If one member of this mass makes contact with me, asking me to carry his excess luggage or enquiring about time-tables, he or she immediately ceases to be classified as humanity in the mass but becomes an individual or person.

There are, of course, individuals also whom I find it hard to love and difficult to believe that God loves. Often my relationships with such people are of a superficial nature, my antipathy preventing closer contact. It has sometimes been my experience to break through this off-putting exterior to the real person behind, to discover what has caused the exterior to be so unattractive and to become more tolerant and understanding, if not actually to get so far as being able to love.

Now the process behind these two examples suggests a principle which I believe to be very true: it is the eye of ignorance which sees people or things in the mass, and all advance in understanding takes the form of breaking some mass up into its component parts – in the case of humanity, into individuals – and further analysing these individuals in terms of the influences that have made them what they are.

It was, I think, Carlyle who told us that genius was 'a transcendent capacity for taking trouble' – in other words, for considering the smallest details. If we are to take seriously the doctrine that man is made in the image of God, our own genius is but a pale reflection of God's. His greatness does not lie in some lofty unconcern with the minutiae of human concern, but precisely in his infinite

capacity for entering into each and every tiny detail. There
is a passage in Matthew 10 about sparrows and the hairs of
our heads being numbered.

An important conclusion from this is that we may derive
fresh confidence from such considerations that it *is* worth
bringing *all* our little quirks and problems before God in
prayer.

APPROACHING THE ENEMY

'What does it really mean – to love your enemy?'

ESSENTIALLY, 'not to rest content with the fact that he
(or she) *is* your enemy.'

I am reminded of a period in my life when my parents
tried, unsuccessfully, to have me taught the piano. When I
was practising I used to strum over the easy bits which I
liked and leave severely alone those difficult passages which
were in fact the only ones which needed practice.

Our relations with other people are often like that. We
naturally gravitate towards those whose company is easy to
us, and avoid those whose company presents any difficulty.

The essence of love is that it never repudiates. What is
a little harder to define is precisely what we mean by
'enemy'.

We can take the word in the sense of opponent. It is
quite inevitable, if you take any active part in human
affairs, that you will find yourself in the opposite camp
from certain others. At this stage, love of them – and,
indeed, love of truth – should lead you to a readiness to
give them a sympathetic hearing. To refuse to hear someone
is to exhibit that fear which is at the opposite pole from
love. It is, after all, extremely unlikely that you are wholly
right and they are wholly wrong.

The next stage of enmity is when there has been
personal insult or animosity. They no longer merely oppose
your *views:* they have got it in for *you*.

Here I Corinthians 13 can come to the rescue. Love is
patient. Love keeps no score of wrongs. Love does not
rejoice in iniquity. The fact is that there are too many
people who positively revel in their enmities. They would be
most disappointed to learn that one of their 'enemies' was
less villainous than they liked to think. Love, on the
contrary, would rejoice in the truth.

But there is another form of enmity which is, to me, infinitely more distressing. It is the enmity of one group against another. It may be the enmity between classes, or it may be racism, or it may be between less clearly defined camps – as when a sudden silence descends upon the patrons of a pub when an outsider appears who is not 'one of them'.

In this context I think that the relevant aspect of love is to treat everyone as an individual. It is in many ways contrary to the ethos of our age to do so. We seem to like pigeon-hole classification today. But love rejects this. It will not accept that you are dealing with a 'manual worker', or a 'toff', or a 'coloured immigrant'. You are dealing with Geoffrey, James and John, each created by God in his own image – and don't you forget it.

PEOPLE AND CAUSES

'In what sense does charity begin at home?'

I AM reminded of a cartoon in an old *Punch* – I think by Tenniel – in which Britannia is depicted observing through a telescope the ill-treatment of African Negroes by non-British Europeans. Her ample bosom is heaving with righteous indignation. Behind her stands a London slum urchin who is tweaking her dress and saying: 'Please, Ma'am; ain't I black enough to be cared for?'

The meaning is clear enough, and it is strangely relevant for today. There is something *suspect* about persons who are indignantly trying to put others to rights when their own household needs to be set in order. There is no necessary equation between having a crack at the South African Government and *really caring* for the Black population.

It seems to me that all the great portrayals of charity, from the well-known Good Samaritan to the delightful picture of Mgr Myriel, the saintly bishop in Victor Hugo's *Les Misérables,* show us someone who is really caring in the context of actual personal encounter – and I think that the value of the saying 'charity begins at home' is that it warns us not to by-pass this first-hand caring in favour of what you might call charity at second-hand – the more impersonal support of causes.

I think also that the words 'at home' can be taken

literally, and that the saying pays tribute to the family as the natural unit in which the members at any rate should be bound together by ties of mutual care and love. This is the most obvious school in which to learn charity.

One can thus depict charity as a series of concentric rings, as on a target, each one deriving its impetus and its quality from the one inside it.

At the centre would be true self-love, and immediately next to it the mutual care of husband and wife; surrounding them, and deriving its quality from their example – the happy family; next comes the extension of family love to those with whom you are brought into personal contact; and finally the outer ring, the support of good causes whose importance you appreciate more fully from your experience of the inner rings.

I do not mean that this is the only picture of charity or that a person who is unmarried or comes from an unhappy family is necessarily defective in charity. Charity may well start elsewhere than in a family, and a family may well become too self-concerned to extend its care beyond its own circle. Sheridan reminded us of this in his *School for Scandal:*

> *'I believe there is no sentiment he hath such faith
> in as that charity begins at home.'*

> *'And his, I presume, is of that domestic sort that
> never stirs abroad.'*

HUMAN VERSUS DIVINE LOVE

*'How is one to take Luke 14:26 : "If any one comes to me and
does not hate his father and mother, wife and children . . .
he cannot be a disciple of mine."?'*

THE TEXT is to me a supreme example of how belittling it is to God's word to treat its language literally without paying it the compliment of careful thought and study.

The passage needs to be interpreted in the light of Matthew 10:37 : 'No man is worthy of me who cares more for father and mother than for me.' Linguistically, 'hate' can mean 'hate by comparison'. Our Lord used to state great principles in bold and paradoxical language. The poet Lovelace did the same when he wrote:

I could not love thee, dear, so much
Loved I not honour more.

I only see the passage as raising with acute urgency the question of the relationship between our love for creatures and our love for the Creator.

Thomas Traherne wrote: 'That violence whereby sometimes a man doteth upon one creature is but a little spark of that Love, even towards all, which lurketh in his nature.' Aldous Huxley commented on this: 'Traherne might have added that 'when we dote upon the perfections and beauties of some one creature' we frequently find ourselves moved to love other creatures. Moreover, to be in love is, in many cases, to have achieved a state of being in which it becomes possible to have direct intuition of the essentially lovely nature of ultimate reality.'

This gets us to the threshold of experiencing the love of God by means of the experience of human love. It is to set our human love in the total context of God's love rather than to allow it to remain an isolated, and therefore meaningless, phenomenon.

Huxley was clearly influenced by Blake, who wrote: 'If the doors of perception were cleansed, everything would appear to man as it is – infinite. For man has closed himself up till he sees all things thro' narrow chinks of his cavern.'

I would not hesitate to claim that love for a human being is one of the most potent forces for 'cleansing the doors of perception'. To return to Huxley, 'The blind are those who are not in love and who therefore fail to see how beautiful the world is and how adorable.' I think that behind this lies the popular saying, 'the whole world loves a lover.'

This is of great pastoral and evangelistic importance. It is at the moment of falling in love that people are most disposed to see the reality of eternity. I wish more clergy would use the opportunity afforded by that dreary legal farce known as 'calling the banns' as an occasion when we all 'rejoice with them that do rejoice' and give thanks for that 'little spark of love' that lies behind the humdrum form.

N.B. I was, I think rightly, accused of not having
answered the question. This article needs to be read in
conjunction with the following one.

THE GREAT COMMANDMENT

'In your article on "hating father and mother" you seem to imply that loving your neighbour comes before loving God. This is the great heresy of today.'

I APOLOGISE if I did not make myself clear. I certainly meant to imply no such thing.

When we say that something 'comes first' we may be referring to priority of importance or to priority in time. The two must not be confused. In suggesting that the experience of human love sometimes comes first in time and prepares the way for our experience of loving God, I was not wishing to suggest that human love was thereby more important.

I agree with you that God - once we have arrived at a recognition of him - must always have priority of importance. God is by definition more important than anything or anyone else. When once we have reached the experience of loving God, then our human loves must flow from this as an inseparable part of it. St John is categorical on this point: 'If a man say, "I love God," and hateth his brother, he is a liar.' Liar is a strong word, but John does not hesitate to use it.

The parallel is fairly close with the relationship of faith to works. I recently claimed that faith is all-important and that works attest the genuineness of our faith. In the same way the first half of our Lord's summary of the law, 'Thou shalt love the Lord thy God,' is all-important; and the second half, 'and thy neighbour as thyself,' attests the genuineness of our love for God.

Christians have made unfortunate attempts to separate these two commandments. Some claim a devotion to God in the sacraments or in prayer or Bible-reading that is somehow valid in the absence of any love towards their neighbour. They have St John's accusation to answer.

Others seem to feel that love towards mankind is sufficient on its own. It is true that these can and do claim the parable of the Sheep and the Goats on their side. 'Anything you did for one of my brothers here, however humble, you did for me.' It is addressed, however, to people who were apparently quite unconscious of having done anything for God at all.

Our Lord's summary remains the rule. Our human loves are greatly enriched by having their source in our love for

God. As Augustine wrote: *Beatus qui amat te, et amicum in in te et inimicum propter te.'* 'Happy is the man who loves you, and his friend in you and his enemy on account of you.'

GLIMPSE OF THE ETERNAL

'We have the commandment to love one another, but it is one which it is impossible to obey.'

LET US START by looking at the difference between love and non-love, and let us be romantic enough to be guided by the poets.

Wordsworth distils all that I mean by non-love into three lines on Peter Bell:

> *A primrose by a river's brim*
> *A yellow primrose was to him*
> *And it was nothing more.*

But to Wordsworth himself such things as primroses were charged with meaning and mystery.

> *There was a time when meadow, grove and stream,*
> *The earth and every common sight*
> *To me did seem*
> *Apparelled in celestial light*
> *The glory and the freshness of a dream.*

For Wordsworth, and for anyone with a spark of poetry in him, nature is always trembling on the brink of the supernatural.

We get the same sense of transfiguration in George Russell looking, in a moment of abstraction, at a handful of sand. 'I suddenly saw the exquisite beauty of every little grain of it ... my consciousness was lighted up from within, and I saw in a vivid way how the whole universe was made up of particles of material which, no matter how dull and lifeless they might seem, were nevertheless filled with this intense and vital beauty.'

The ordinary suddenly being seen as the extraordinary with a consciousness 'lighted up from within' and 'apparelled in celestial light' so as to reveal a previously unperceived beauty or meaning: that seems to me to be a process closely akin to the experience of nascent love.

The question must now be asked: 'is the poet merely seeing nature through artificial, rose-tinted spectacles, or is he vouchsafed a glimpse of the real truth?' I would stake everything on the connection between this transfigured vision and eternal truth. It seems to me that the person we love most is the person we understand most; that love and truth go hand in hand. I find, with very few exceptions, that the deeper I get in relationship with someone the easier it is to love them.

In this context the obstacle to love is neither hate nor fear (the traditional opposites), but detachment. I sometimes used to find when visiting that after even perhaps an hour of conversation one went away feeling that no contact had been made at a meaningful level. Then, perhaps, something happened - an accident, an illness, an engagement; the barriers were down; real self got through to real self, and the process of love and understanding could begin.

I can only say: 'keep open to it, keep praying, and never be satisfied with less than love.'

MOMENT OF BREAKTHROUGH

'We are commanded to love, but love is not at my command.'

YOU cannot, of course, force yourself to feel an emotion which does not come naturally to you, but you may be able to remove certain obstacles to love, so that you are at least disposed to love your fellow men. This raises in my mind the question of what place emotion has in *agape*.

Although we are called to love all mankind, we cannot enjoy the same degree of intimacy with all. I see within the term *Christian Love* a series of concentric rings.

I think that love is in the first place a recognition of fact: that this person is made by God and loved by God; it is a recognition that he matters to God as much as I do, that his welfare is as important as mine. So the first, or outer ring is expressed in the saying: 'Love worketh no ill to his neighbour.' That, I believe, is at your command.

But St Peter takes us a lot further when he says: 'Love one another with a pure heart *fervently*. The Greek word for fervently - *ektenos* - suggests a reaching out towards the other person.

I have often found that St Paul's injunction to 'rejoice with them that do rejoice and weep with them that weep' has provided the occasion for entering into a deeper personal relationship with them – for reaching out to them. By sharing a bridegroom's joy or a widow's sorrow I have been drawn into the reality of that person's life. I use the word 'reality' because one of the definitions of love that has interested me is that it consists in the recognition that the other person really exists. This is the inner ring.

We obviously have a unique awareness of our own existence. There are people who seem to stop short at this and regard other people as an audience to play to, or as pawns to be pushed around, or obstacles to be removed in a game of power.

If you want to cultivate the relationship of love, it is a good plan to look out for the poignant moments in a person's life – the moments of deep emotion, the moments when they stand upon the threshold of one of the great adventures of life. I have already instanced marriage; it might be a young man at his ordination or a boy on his first day at school, or a woman when she first knows she is to be a mother. You may, in appropriate circumstances, suddenly remember how you felt on those occasions in your own life, and realize that they are feeling the same, and the breakthrough occurs. A dispassionate concern for the welfare of others becomes a deep and personal relationship. You are more likely to make this breakthrough if you regularly pray for them.

A PROPER PRIDE

'We are told to love our neighbours as ourselves; what does loving oneself really mean?'

I WISH more attention had been given to this in Christian thought. There has been plenty of grovelling self-abasement – 'we worms of earth' – but with how much sincerity I am not in a position to judge.

There have been sweeping condemnations of pride which have, however, omitted to think out the borderline between pride and proper pride. How seldom we even hear the phrase 'proper pride'. We do at least hear it sometimes in French, but even *amour propre* can be used in the sense of conceit.

If I were translating *amour propre* into English I would in most cases put 'self-respect', but it would be correctly rendered 'pride' in such a context as 'he took a pride in his work.' Now I believe that no objection could be made to someone taking a pride in his work. Indeed, if more people could do this, the world would be a much happier place.

It partakes of pride, for the feeling could be experienced as 'Dunlop doesn't stoop to shoddy work like that: do it properly.' It need not, however, partake of the sin of pride, though it obviously entails sailing very near the wind. Proper pride can easily become self-glorification; but, insofar as the locus of pride is in the excellence of the work and not in the credit reflected on the workman, it is a healthy condition.

Self-love is this same craftsman's pride, but in that work of art in which we are all engaged – the shaping of our own characters and lives. Just as the good craftsman would not stoop to shoddy work, so the artist of his life who is inspired by self-love does not stoop to shoddy behaviour.

Not long ago I wrote in one of my articles on the declining moral standards of this present age, and I suggested that the centre of gravity was in the decline of personal probity. This I would now instance as a typical example of the want of self-love. If you love your child, you do not tolerate his becoming a thief or an artful dodger. If you love yourself, you would not tolerate such standards in yourself either.

I have described this as sailing close to the wind. But righteousness is always next-door to self-righteousness, and true self-love would always be on its guard against pharisaism as much as any other sin. As so often in ethics the decisive question is that of motive, and I would suggest as a legitimate motive *contribution to the creative environment.* What *you* are affects the way in which *others* develop.

If we could see that our personal (and what we might think private) standards of morality *are* our contribution to society, we would find a new depth of meaning in Alexander Pope's assertion: 'true self-love and social are the same.'

N.B. The quotation is from Pope's Essay on Man.

DEGREES OF 'HATE'

'In saying that we cannot love God, whom we can't see,
unless we love our brothers, whom we can see, Jesus
sets a fantastic standard; to see some people is to hate
them.'

I THINK it would be worth your while trying to analyse
what you mean by 'hate'. There are probably elements of
prejudice – often caused by difference of class, race or
ideology; there could be physical revulsion; there could be
moral disapproval; deepest of all, there could be fear – fear
that in some way this person constitutes a threat to you
and your cherished way of life.

But I believe that often we use the word 'hate' when we
really mean something more like 'I can't be doing with him.'
Perhaps 'antipathy' is the right word. And 'antipathy'
immediately gives us a clear opposite which is 'sympathy' –
quite literally, 'to enter into the deepest feelings' of
someone else.

If one of these people whom you hate were badly injured
before your eyes, I believe that you might feel sympathy
for all your hatred. Instead of being aware of the
differences between yourself and the other person, you
would become aware of your common humanity.

This brings me to one of my favourite defitions of love,
which comes from Simone Weil – 'belief in the existence of
other human beings as such'. Certainly the moment you do
begin to recognize a common humanity you are well on the
way towards love.

It is, of course, intrinsically unlikely that many of those
you hate will be injured in your sight. I merely used that
as an illustration. Berdyaev gives us an alternative way of
attaining this end:

> *'Our attitude to all men would be Christian if we*
> *regarded them as though they were dying, and*
> *determined our relation to them in the light of*
> *death, both of their death and of our own. A*
> *person who is dying calls forth a special kind of*
> *feeling. Our attitude to him is at once softened*
> *and lifted up to a higher plane. We can then feel*
> *compassion for people whom we did not love. But*
> *every man is dying; I too am dying and must*
> *never forget about death.'* ·

That is to look at others in the light of eternity, which is the same as to look at them in the light of God. It is only in that light that we are likely to attain the 'reverence for life' which is necessary if our full capacity for loving is to be realized.

A GIFT FREELY BESTOWED

'We get overfamiliar with certain "words of piety" and tend to ignore their meaning. What do we mean by grace?'

THE FUNDAMENTAL MEANING of 'grace' is that of a gift, unmerited and unearned. It is freely bestowed and could perfectly well be withheld.

The Greek word is *charis;* and the gifts of the Holy Spirit, like the gift of teaching or the gift of putting the deepest knowledge into words, are thus *charismata.* The word has a very much wider application than is commonly given to 'charismatic'.

One of the most difficult, but one of the most liberating, conceptions of the Christian faith is that we have no claims on God's good will and no ability to climb the ladder of desert. Our position is that of sinners who have been forgiven when in fact we deserve punishment. But God 'has not dealt with us after our sins, nor rewarded us according to our wickedness.' Instead of exacting retribution, he has borne our sin in the person of Jesus Christ on the Cross.

This is the ultimate length to which love can go; this is the fundamental 'Good News' of the gospel. It can only be good news to those who have sufficient awareness of their sin to feel its liberation. Those who respond, answering love with love, are receiving God's *grace* - God's free gift. The liberation which they experience is the essence of salvation. The fundamental idea behind the Hebrew word of salvation is 'to be wide', 'to develop without hindrance'. Grace removes the inhibiting forces.

Mankind, however, is peculiarly resistant to this idea. Within the Church there is still plenty of opposition to the doctrine that salvation comes from faith alone. There is a deep-set feeling that it is somehow immoral and that men should get their deserts. Naturally this feeling is more attractive to those who think they have attained a standard that deserves praise. Such people tend to be more harsh in their condemnation of those who seem to deserve punishment.

George Bernard Shaw once said: 'Virtue does not consist in abstaining from vice but in not desiring it.' I once quoted this to a friend who thought for a bit and then responded: 'If virtue consists in doing what we desire, where is the merit in it?' Christians can quite happily answer: 'There is no merit in it, thank God.'

The proper response to a gift is thanksgiving. Thanksgiving acknowledges the origin of the gift and is therefore the antidote to pride. It is quite illogical to be proud of having received an unmerited gift.

SECTION 3

Sin

INTOLERABLE SIN

'How can we be helped to say with sincerity when recalling our offences: "the burden of them is intolerable"?'

IT IS significant that the words occur in a *general* confession. You can regard that act as a number of individuals making their private confessions simultaneously, and you can regard it as the corporate confession of a corporate failure. It is easier to see sin as intolerable when you see it as a corporate defect in the human race.

You have only to look at the world today to see hatred, distrust and indifference bedevilling almost everything we do; warfare, and that armed neutrality which does not deserve the name of peace; violence in all its forms - class strife, racial strife, industrial strife. It is appalling that human beings are so seldom able to settle their differences amicably.

Then look at some local situation. It seems that in almost any village or local community you will find endless little private feuds - Mrs Jones not speaking to Mrs Smith because of some fancied insult years ago; people taking offence when no offence was meant; marriages that have come unstuck; friendships that have been broken. There is no end to the petty impediments to happy and harmonious relationships.

I am not talking about crimes as a lawyer would understand the word; I am talking about ordinary (I was about to say 'decent') people; about the 'crimes' of greed, selfishness, hypocrisy and pride - and against such there is no statutory law.

Then look at the other side - the extraordinary capacity of man to be noble. You will find examples of long-suffering and self-sacrifice which leave you humbled and chastened; the sweet, unselfish nature of *this* person; the sparklingly happy atmosphere of *that* family; the smooth-running of this particular enterprise where personal relations have been good. We *can* do it, make no mistake about that. But so often we just *don't*. It is not a situation one should be content to tolerate. It is intolerable.

But what of the individual? I notice that you use the word 'offences'. It is a word which I distrust in connection with confession. So many of us do not commit *offences*. But sin means failure to reach our target. We must take seriously our own share in the corporate failure, and not tolerate anything but the best in ourselves. It is not easy to judge the individual's share in corporate sin. When a Frenchman pointed at me and said, 'You burned Joan of Arc!' I did not feel able in any way to accept responsibility for that incident. But we have all got some responsibility for the situation today. There is a very true remark in *Oliver Twist* when Bill Sykes' accomplice, Nancy, says to Rose: 'O Lady, Lady; if there were more like you, there be fewer like me. There would, there would.' It is up to each of us to see that there *are* more like Rose.

BETTER THAN OTHERS?

*'A bishop recently told the CMS to "get rid of the last
lingering thoughts that we are better than others." If a
Christian is no better than a non-Christian, why bother to
be one?'*

THERE SEEMS to be a real paradox here. The New
Testament is quite explicit. Christianity is the Way, the
Truth and the Life. For those who have embraced the Way,
their new life is painted in sharp contra-distinction to their
former vicious habits.

A life liberated by the redeeming power of Christ,
surrendered to God in love and continually directed by the
Holy Spirit, bringing peace and joy to the individual and
inspiring him with love for his fellows, is how we are *meant*
to live: any falling short of that is sin. Translate this into
ethical terms, and this is the *right* way to live: it is *better*
than any that falls short of it.

And yet, for people whose feet *are* set along this path,
to be consciously thinking they are better is highly
distasteful. The Pharisee was, in ethical terms, 'better'
than the Publican. Why did the latter go home justified?

I have said before that it is quite meaningless to say of
any two people, 'this man is better than that man.' It is
precisely here that I would interpose our Lord's words,
'Judge not, lest ye be judged.' We are warned elsewhere
that God does not judge as we do. Perhaps an illustration
would make this clear.

When I was at my preparatory school, I was a bad
runner. My parents, however, arrived on Sports Day in the
middle of the race, and were pleased and surprised to see
me leading the field. They naturally concluded that I was
the best runner. They were wrong. They were arguing
from a faulty premiss because they thought all the boys had
started even. As a matter of fact it was a handicap race,
and I was leading because I had started well out in front.
The best runner was in reality somewhere at the back.

I regard life as a handicap race, and for the most part
we do not know each other's handicaps. Because I am
apparently morally 'better' than someone else, that does not
mean that in God's eyes I am doing any more than maintain
the lead given by my natural advantages. Someone 'behind'
me who started with all the odds against him may be
putting up a far better show.

But perhaps your real answer is to be found in the nature of love. A Christian is not told to *be* good: he is told to *have* love, and a person genuinely activated by love would not in fact be looking inwards at himself and thinking: 'I must be *better* than those who have less love.' Love does not think that way.

THE SIN OF PRIDE

'Which is the root sin, pride or (cf. H.A. Williams) diffidence?'

I AM not quite happy about your word 'diffidence'. As I understand H.A. Williams he means a refusal, conscious or unconscious, to become your full self, to become what you are capable of becoming.

There is a story of a schoolboy who was angrily approached by his headmaster with the demand, 'What are you doing?' 'Nothing, Sir,' answered the boy, all injured innocence. 'Well, you are not here to do nothing!' thundered the headmaster, and set him a hundred lines.

I think this story might contain an image of the Last Judgement. Virtue does not consist in committing no offences. It is something positive and involves reaching out to the fullest extent of one's ability. Anything short of that is sin.

But I doubt whether failure to be our full selves is always diffidence. There may be areas of potential expansion which are sealed off from us by fear and which could be opened up by love. A lot of people I can think of, for instance, would become fuller personalities if they learned to move more freely in other social circles than that to which their birth and education tend to confine them.

But just as often these self-limitings proceed from self-satisfaction. There can be no more effective block to progress than contentment with your present position - and this contentment is a form of pride.

Where fear and pride are concerned, it is not easy to say which is the chicken and which is the egg. Do we resort to pride in order to bolster ourselves up when deep down we know we are afraid? Or are we afraid, precisely, that to venture outside our present little scheme of life would be to expose ourselves to a whole series of affronts to our pride?

While I agree with H.A. Williams that refusal to become

one's full self is of the essence of sin, and that this is often caused by the sort of fear which love casts out, I stick to the traditional view that pride is the cardinal sin, and for this reason. Pride is almost by definition unlikely to see any need for improvement. Fear is more likely to be recognized as inadequacy, and that is the first step towards its removal.

DIFFERENT SORTS OF PRIDE

'Why do moral theologians regard pride as the greatest sin?'

IT IS a healthy form of self-examination to ask yourself whether you think of yourself primarily in terms of those things which distinguish you from other people or in terms of those which you have in common with them. The sins of pride and hardness of heart are likely to grow in the former half of your garden, whereas the virtues of humility, compassion and forgiveness thrive only in the latter.

The German playwriter Ernst Toller wrote in his *Letters from Prison*: 'I am only the vessel in which the powers of life work, and create; and I dare not but be humble at the little I can manage to let come through.' As a writer he was sensitive to the compulsion of unrecognized forces behind the actions of men. To the Christian, the 'powers of life' can be identified with God, and pride becomes the taking of credit to oneself for things which could and should be attributed to Him.

There are, of course, many degrees of pride, and not all of them are equally serious offences. G.K. Chesterton wrote in his book, *The Heretics*: 'the one kind of pride which is wholly damnable is the pride of a man who has something to be proud of. The pride which, proportionately speaking, does not hurt the character, is the pride in things which reflect no credit on the person at all.

'Thus it does a man no harm to be proud of his country, and comparatively little harm to be proud of his remote ancestors. It does him more harm to be proud of having made money, because in that he has a little more reason for pride. It does him more harm still to be proud of what is nobler than money - intellect. And it does him most harm of all to value himself for the most valuable thing on earth - goodness.'

There are many sins which are as it were peripheral to one's central character. This is often true of the so-called 'sins of the flesh', which can co-exist with a warm-hearted generosity. But pride is central to a man's character and will nullify his potential virtues. As Chesterton points out, the worst form is pride in one's own virtue. It has the deadly quality of turning virtue into vice.

I would regard as virtues the qualities which enable people to live together in harmony. But pride is by its very nature divisive. One of the terms most used in advertising is 'exclusive,' which appeals directly to pride and is an abominable reason for wanting anything.

The antidote to pride is often thanksgiving. Any gift which we possess is potentially a ground for distinguishing us from our fellows. But once it is recognized as a gift - which I am sure is what Chesterton was thinking of when he mentions intellect - it is recognized as coming from a source outside ourselves. This is, of course, implicit in thanksgiving.

SETTING US FREE FROM SIN

'In what sense does the truth set us free?'

IT IS CLEAR from the context of your quotation (John 8) that the freedom envisaged is freedom from sin. In one verse it is the truth that is the liberating force; in another it is Jesus himself. Elsewhere John makes the identification explicit in the statement, 'I am the Truth.' We are on to a vast subject, and I can only give a few pointers in this space.

There is an old saying, derived from Burns: 'if we could see ourselves as others see us.' If only we could. It would help us to follow St Paul's injunction to the Romans not to think too highly of ourselves but to 'think our way to a sober estimate.' How many of the sins of pride could be shaken off!

But how much more so if we could see ourselves as God sees us. If we could once gain this vision, then true humility would be ours, for neither pride, which overestimates our importance, nor false humility, which likes to grovel in phrases such as 'worms of earth' or 'frail and trembling sheep,' would retain any hold upon us.

I think I am right in saying that much of the work of

the psychoanalyst consists in trying to get the patient to
bring to conscious level, and face up to, truths which were
originally found too hard to face and driven into the
sub-conscious. This would be an example of truth
liberating. It also has the value of helping us to see sin as
something inhibiting and cramping which prevents us from
filling out into the fullness of the glorious liberty of the
sons of God. So often sin is only conceived in terms of the
little lists of peccadilloes so dear to the compilers of
manuals for confession.

The converse application of this principle is in its
application to our estimate not of ourselves but of other
people. I rather hesitate to use the word 'snobbery',
because I think that popular imagination has narrowed this
word down to the attitude of those who collect titled people
or indulge in name-dropping. The barriers of class must be
seen from both sides as factors inhibiting fellowship.

All snobbery, in this wider sense, is an offence against
truth. It puts a false value in place of the true value,
which is a person's worth in the sight of God. There is a
very real freedom in the person who moves easily and mixes
easily at all social levels. Once we can learn to regard
others as what they are - children created by God loved by
God and redeemed by God - we have broken a bondage.

Perhaps one of the deepest insights comes from those
regimes, whether Fascist or Communist or anything else,
which find it necessary to suppress the truth in order to
maintain power. *They* know that truth would set their
people free. Hence the important maxim that education
teaches you *how* to think while propaganda tells you *what*
to think.

TRUE REPENTANCE

*'Cardinal Newman once said that the true penitent never
forgives himself: is this so?'*

IT SEEMS a very odd thing to have said. In the first place
I think it is a misuse of the word *forgive*. The question is
not whether we forgive ourselves, but whether God forgives
us; and there is not much point in his doing that if we are
not going to accept his forgiveness.

There is a great difference between repenting of a sin
and harping on it. The latter could very well only lead to a

guilt complex. There was some excellent teaching on the subject in the rabbinical writings. 'If anyone has committed a serious sin, let him beware thinking of it ... turn away from evil, hold it not in remembrance ... resolve today from the depth of your heart and in a joyful mood to abstain from sin and do good.'

In Christian writing we find the same idea taken a stage further. Walter Hylton, whose meditations *The Scale of Perfection* were published by Evelyn Underhill, gives us the advice: 'When thou attackest the root of sin, fix thy thought more upon the God whom thou desirest than upon the sin which thou abhorrest.' There speaks not only an unusually perceptive Christian, but an extremely sound psychologist. I remember the late Dr William Brown telling me that the only way to get rid of a temptation was to turn the mind to some positive good. This idea of turning the mind is the essential point.

I think that there is often the wrong image created by the word *repentance*. I suspect that in many minds it conjures up the picture of somebody dressed in sackcloth and ashes and beating his breast. This is remorse - literally 'biting again'. It is the backlash of conscience and it may very well bring about repentance, but repentance itself is something bigger. It means, in the original Greek, a mental right-about turn, a change in the inner man. It may start in sorrow, but the rabbi I have just quoted was right in emphasizing that it proceeds in 'a joyful mood'.

I would suggest, for the image of repentance, the picture of a motorist who has taken the wrong road. For some time he may continue in the vain hope that things will turn out all right, but the time comes when he puts on the brakes, reverses the car and says: 'We're going back to where we left the main road.' There may be a period of self-reproach, but the final emotion should be one of relief at being back once more on the right road. Repentance is the homing instinct of the moral man.

SINS OF THE FLESH

'The last words of the epistle for Advent 1, "give no more thought to the bodily appetites," cannot be obeyed. We must eat to live.'

FOR THIS PASSAGE I prefer the translation of the

Authorised Version: 'make no provision for the flesh to
fulfil the lusts thereof.' There is, as you imply, such a
thing as a healthy appetite, and you may be thinking of the
right use of sex as well as of food.

There are two comments I would like to make. The first
is that the word 'flesh' covers a far wider field than is
commonly supposed. It is not to be confined to the physical
body. In I Corinthians 3:3 (NEB), we read: 'you are still
on the merely natural plane.' The AV gives: 'you are yet
carnal.'

The Greek word *sarx*, often translated 'flesh' is
rendered by the words in italics. But the passage goes on
to describe this 'carnal' or 'fleshly' behaviour, instancing
'jealousy, strife and divisions' - the latter being the sort of
faction-mongering that would claim 'I am of Paul' or 'I am of
Apollos.'

It is important to realize that jealousy, strife and
faction-mongering are just as much 'sins of the flesh' as
gluttony or lechery. I think that we can take the term 'the
flesh' to mean the whole human personality minus any
activity of the Spirit.

My second comment concerns the word translated
'appetite' (NEB) or 'lust' (AV), for which latter I have
expressed my preference. The Greek word transliterates
epithumia. It is morally neutral and only means 'a very
strong desire'. That it can be wholly good is proved by the
use of this word by St Luke (22:15) of Jesus' longing to
share the Last Supper with his disciples. Even the English
word 'lust' can properly denote pleasure and delight,
deriving as it does from the German *lustig.* There is no
moral reprobation about the phrase 'young and lusty as an
eagle'.

In the passage to which you refer, however, the word
'lust' is clearly used in a pejorative sense. It means 'those
strong desires which are illegitimate' and would include
such passions as envy, hatred and covetousness.

It is interesting to recall that this passage played a
decisive part in the conversion of St Augustine. He records
how he was walking in his garden, 'brooding in despair
over his futile struggles to live a good life,' when he heard
a voice like that of a child singing which bade him, 'take
up and read.' He opened the Bible at random, and this
passage was the first that met his eyes. 'With the end of
that sentence, as though the light of assurance had poured
into my heart, all the shades of doubt were scattered.'

ARE INFANTS INVOLVED IN SIN?

*'What does the new baptism service for infants mean by
"receiving forgiveness of all their sins"?'*

IT IS PARTLY a question of whether you regard baptism as
conferring a status or initiating a process. I am reminded
of those who used to ask me shortly after my wedding,
'And how do you like the married state?' I was sometimes
pedantic enough to correct them and say: 'Do you mean the
marriage process?'

It is a pedantry, however, about which I am serious.
The idea of married life as status – which suggests
something static if not stagnant – is not to be encouraged.
Without the emphasis on continuing process it may well
become an empty, meaningless relationship.

I think that the same is true of baptism and the
Christian living which ought to proceed from it. It is not
enough to think of it as the conferring of status; it is the
initiation of the whole process of dying to sin and rising to
righteousness (as St Paul said: 'I die daily') of which the
forgiveness of sins is an inseparable part. The baptismal
rite symbolizes this whole process. In one important sense,
therefore, the forgiveness of sins is forward-looking.

We must now ask: 'Is there a sense in which, even for
infants, we can think of sin as something not of which they
are already *guilty*, but in which they are already involved?'

I doubt if many people today could accept the doctrine
of original sin as it was worked out by St Augustine. But
there is a trend in modern thought which suggests a new
approach to original sin. We ask with a new emphasis,
'Which of the two sinned; this man or his parents?' And of
course the same shift of responsibility can be made on
behalf of the parents and their parents and so on, until the
whole human race (Adam?) is comprehended. Today we
readily find the origins of man's shortcomings in his human
heredity and his human environment, any product of which
may be, in the words of the 1928 Prayer Book, 'by birth
prone to sin.'

But, if responsibility for this proneness to sin is shared
with the human race aṣ a whole, so responsibility for the
re-orientation of the child towards God (repentance) may lie
initially with the strongest creative force in his life – his
own family circle. In this way, I think, we can make sense
of an act of vicarious repentance.

I do not mean by this to suggest that there is no place at a later date for individual responsibility for sin and a need for personal repentance. But both the words *sin* and *repentance* cover a wider field than individual wrong-doing and individual re-orientation towards God.

CAN SIN BE DELIBERATE?

'The phrase in the Series 3 confession, "through our own deliberate fault", offends me. Hebrews 10:26 states that deliberate sin is not forgiveable.'

I HOLD no brief for the use of this phrase in the confession, and I would like to hear it defended by one of the Liturgical Commission. I believe deliberate sin to be a rarity.

Just consider what 'deliberate' means. The verb *to deliberate* means to debate - to weigh one thing against another and to arrive at a thought-out conclusion. I doubt if any of my own sins have been the outcome of such a process - the decision, after careful deliberation, to do what one knows is wrong. And this could, of course, be the sin against the Holy Spirit: the rejecting of his guidance.

It seems to me that the deliberation, if it takes place at all, is more likely to be a process in which one kids oneself for the time being that what one wants to do is perfectly all right. But far more often there is no deliberation at all. You just find you've done it - which so often means *said it* - or that you just have not done it (the sins of omission), and the action was spontaneous and not deliberate.

The process was described by William Temple in these words: 'I did it, and what made me do it was myself.' In other words, actions are predestined by character. And what has formed my character? Here Temple answers that the formative influence is the habitual focusing of the attention on good or evil. Hence the importance of St Paul's injunction: 'whatsoever things are good ... think on these things.'

A great deal of my sin is not only not deliberate; it is not even my fault. The picture of sin that I get from the New Testament - and especially from the words used of the forgiveness of sin - is far more like a prison that I have been locked into and to which our Lord throws open the door.

But we must be careful not to go too far to the opposite extreme. I am not refusing to accept *any* responsibility for my actions. We all, I believe, have some share in the responsibility. I would not wish to substitute 'Dear me, my parents must have been misguided' for 'God be merciful to me, a sinner.' But I do not think that the phrases in any confession known to me do justice to the complex nature of sin and the even more complex background of responsibility.

USES OF CONFESSION

'Is it not regrettable that the practice of auricular confession is so little insisted upon today?'

THIS QUESTION should have been asked of someone with more experience of hearing confessions than I have. Most priests observe a reticence about what they have heard in the confessional, even when no names are mentioned, so one is not often able to profit by the experience of others.

Although I have heard some confessions, it has not often been my privilege to hear one that I felt worthwhile. I believe that some people go about it in a very mistaken manner, and I am further convinced of this by certain little manuals which I have seen – lists of suggested peccadilloes of the most pretentious triviality. I forget if I actually saw 'wasted any bits of string?', or if my aunt invented it, but it is not far wide of the mark.

Apart from being pure pharisaism, this sort of thing seems to be a deliberate diversion of the attention from the areas that really matter – a scraping off of a few pimples when the whole bloodstream is in need of purifying.

I dare say that there are some good manuals; I am sure that there are some excellent spiritual directors. But I have no doubt that the essential business of both is to direct the penitent's attention to his true motives for action and to the real reasons for which he holds those opinions which control his actions. This approach would help to break what seems to me to be a tacit assumption that the penitent's only area of concern is that dark side of his own life which he recognizes as sin.

Alas, it is not so simple as that. If you really want to get at the truth about yourself – and that is the ultimate

object of the exercise of confession, since it is the truth
that sets us free - you must learn to scrutinize also what
you imagine to be your virtues.

Recently I wrote an article on the merits of kindness. I
stick to what I said: this is one of the great virtues. But
it can be a fairly devastating experience to examine the
motives behind some of your kindest actions. To what
extent, for instance, do you give priority to the things
that belong not to your peace but to your vanity? It is
pleasant, not to say flattering, to know that you are
building up a reputation of being 'a very kind person'.

But here there is another danger: it does not do to get
too complicated. A quick laugh at yourself and back to your
kindness please! But I am straying from my subject. I
believe that the role of the confessional would be in less
disrepute in certain circles if it were thought to concern
itself more with the essential realities than with trivialities
such as I have mentioned above.

SECTION 4

Ethics

STRAIT & NARROW

'In what sense is Christianity "the strait and narrow way"?'

THE WORD 'narrow' is not, at first impact, attractive. It
suggests something like narrow-mindedness - the limitations
imposed upon those who can never rise high enough to see
the broader horizons of life. The mental image evoked by
the word is of something like a deep railway cutting, with
high banks on either side shutting out truth and
experience. If you have a subconscious mental image of that
sort, you start with a prejudice.

So let us change the image. A narrow path need not be
at the bottom of a trough; it can be on the ridge of a

mountain. Since I spend most of my holidays in Skye I can easily see the 'strait and narrow' as a striding ridge of the Cuillins. It at once becomes something attractive, exhilarating, challenging. No restricted horizons here – you have the freedom of an extremely broad outlook.

But you are obliged to keep to your narrow path, for on either side the ground falls abruptly away in a steep and treacherous slope.

If this strait and narrow path is the Christian life, then one of those slopes may be labelled 'sin' and the other 'self-righteousness'. There is no gain in avoiding the one if your evasive action causes you to fall down the other.

If I had to choose I would prefer to avoid self-righteousness. Wrong-doing is straight-forward, and often brings its own nemesis and its own route to repentance. Our Lord found the tarts and touts of Palestine plain sailing compared with the Pharisees. Self-righteousness is the corruption of something good, which it twists into pride and selfishness and vindictiveness, which are bad. What is more, it puts other people off righteousness, for which they often mistake it.

But somewhere between the two is the path of single-minded virtue, and by 'single-minded' I mean virtue which proceeds from a pure motive. We so often act from a mixture of motives.

Take an example: suppose that I see a child drowning – my first instinct might be to rush into the water and save it; my second, remembering my poor performance as a swimmer, to go and *get* help. Another cry from the water might renew the note of compassion and recall me to the brink in an agony of indecision. I would never cease to reproach myself if the child died (note the self-regarding element).

Then a new idea darts into my mind. The headlines flash out: 'Palace Investiture for Country Parson. Suffolk Vicar gets G.C.' In I go – and who is to say from what motive? But now imagine the same situation if that child were my own. I would go straight into the water.

Love by-passes these complications of motive. I suspect that the strait-and-narrow is the Way of Love.

RULES & REGULATIONS

*'Christianity seems to be based on a lot of negative commands,
all beginning: "Thou shalt not ... ".'*

SO DOES cricket. 'Thou shalt not allow the ball to hit thy
wicket. Thou shalt not prevent the ball from hitting thy
wicket by placing thy leg before it. ...' You might amuse
yourself by trying to complete the decalogue.

There is a curious aversion to rules these days,
especially if they are in negative form, and I think that
this must come from a failure to understand their purpose.

It is sometimes thought that a relaxation of the rules
would contribute to the general enjoyment, and that those
who enforce rules are therefore hard-hearted killjoys. But
just imagine an umpire at cricket who kept on relaxing the
rules. 'Poor old chap – he couldn't help having his leg
before the wicket. Everybody does it these days. Who made
these rules, anyway? What right has the MCC to lay down
the law?' etc. This man would not be increasing the
pleasure to be obtained from cricket. He would be
destroying it completely.

Rules are not arbitrary methods of spoiling the fun:
they are the indispensable means whereby the general
standard of enjoyment may be maintained. If you seek the
general enjoyment of the two teams, you will uphold the
rules. It may well involve temporary hardship to the
individual. It is no fun to be out first ball.

This is not to say that all rules must be in all cases
enforced. Some rules are bad rules and ought to be
changed. But it is necessary to remember that rules nearly
always rely upon the authority of experience and not of
reason.

I doubt if anyone would arrive at the present rules of
cricket by the pure use of his reason, and a rationalist
watching the game for the first time might easily fail to see
the reason for some of the rules. But generations of
cricketers have found by experience that these rules are
conducive to the best, and therefore the most enjoyable
game. You can usually only criticize as the result of long
experience.

By and large, this is true also of the Game of Life. The
rules are rules for a good, and therefore an enjoyable, life.
They often have to penalize the individual for the general
good.

But it is not true to say that Christianity *is* based on negative commands. Our Lord's summary of the Law is positive. 'Love God, love your neighbour.' Many of the other commands in the New Testament – 'be kind,' 'forgive,' 'be generous' are in positive form, but of course they entail a negative counterpart: 'Do not be *un*kind,' 'Do not be *un*forgiving,' 'Do not be mean.' Does it really matter if some of them come out in their negative form?

MORALS & MOTIVES

'How is one to interpret the term "do-gooder"?'

THERE CAN be no doubt that in current usage this phrase is meant to be anything but complimentary. When justly applied, it is nothing less than the world's rejection of morality without love. It is the tragedy of morality that, the higher we climb, the brighter the light and so the darker the shadow. It is fatally easy to pass from 'a good deed to be done' to 'ME doing a good deed.'

Unless you learn to be vigilant and introspective you can reach a state in which your so-called morality is just a somewhat rarefied form of selfishness, in which case a condescending or patronizing manner will often betray the fact and earn you the unwelcome title of 'do-gooder'. It is this fact which enables the cynic to doubt, and not without some plausibility, the very possibility of dis-interested good works.

That arch-cynic the Duc de la Rochefoucauld challenged the virtuous man *'de faire sans témoins ce qu'on serait capable de faire devant tout le monde'* (to do without witnesses what you could do before the eyes of all). His thinking here is, no doubt unintentionally, in line with that of Jesus Christ: 'Do not your alms before men.'

Yet even this test is not rigorous enough. To some people it matters more to be virtuous in their own eyes than in the sight of men. There could still be a self-satisfaction in knowing that you had denied yourself the more obvious reward of a shining reputation.

Another test is this: suppose that you are moved to do some act of kindness to someone else, and you find that another person has got in before you and done it ... are you disappointed? If you had no selfish motive, you would be simply glad that this particular need had been met.

I remember vividly the only time I have pulled the communication cord on a train. An elderly lady had failed to board the carriage and was dragged off the platform still clinging to the door handle. Any desire I may have had to help her was eclipsed by my frantic fear that someone else might get to the communication cord before I did!

All these problems, however, disappear when love enters on the scene. Had the lady been my wife or my daughter, I would have had a single-minded desire for her safety.

Having said all this, I should add that it doesn't do to be too complicated about motives. I can imagine conscientious readers now refraining from acts of kindness for fear that their motives were impure! The answer to such people is to get on and do whatever conscience demands. Over-scrupulosity is but another form of self-centredness.

RIGHT TO BE HAPPY

'I feel guilty about being happy in a world where there is so much poverty.'

GUILTY OF *what*? And would your *un*-happiness be of the slightest benefit to those who are less fortunate? These are the questions that will take you to the heart of the matter.

If you had said that you felt guilty about being rich in a world of poverty, then the answer would be plain sailing. There is a connection between wealth and poverty; but I wonder if there is any value in contrasting two such unconnected things as happiness and poverty. I do not think that happiness has much to do with material conditions. It was recorded of Bonhoeffer that he radiated happiness in the prisons of the Gestapo.

There is an interesting approach to the subject in the writings of André Gide. He makes, essentially, three points: 1 - 'I feel in myself an imperative obligation to be happy'; 2 - 'I need the happiness of all in order to be happy myself'; 3 - 'Any happiness which can only be had at the expense of another seems to be detestable.'

How do we reconcile the last two with the first?

You will notice that in the last one he seems to have given a rather more 'materialistic' meaning to the word happiness, and this forces us to consider the ingredients of our happiness, and perhaps to reject some which are by nature exclusive. But, if I am right in saying that there is not much connection between happiness and material conditions, then the third point will not often apply.

Take an obvious example – a really successful marriage. It satisfies Gide's third point in that it is clearly at no one else's expense. Why should *you* feel guilty about *your* marriage just because others have made a mess of theirs? There is no connection between your happiness and their unhappiness; there is no cause for guilt, and there would be no gain from the surrender of your happiness.

On the contrary (and this is where Gide's first point comes in) if you consider the force of example and the fact that true happiness tends to be infectious, you might well feel an obligation to cultivate something which would be an inspiration to others. You would thus be going as far as it is possible to go towards the satisfaction of Gide's second point: 'I need the happiness of all.'

But, although this may provide a salutary consideration, it will not do as an absolute condition. Taken rigorously, it would deprive everyone of the possibility of being happy; and who would be the gainer then?

GOD'S LAW AND MAN'S NATURE

'Has the Church the right to impose Christian moral standards on unbelievers?'

THIS IS A very important and far-reaching question, and it requires a thorough investigation of the nature of moral standards.

I often get the impression that these are regarded as being similar in kind to the sort of arbitrary restrictions on our liberty which a headmaster (perhaps I should say an old-fashioned headmaster) might impose upon his pupils – laws which one obeys out of prudence, or disobeys if one is so constituted as to enjoy challenging authority.

God's laws are more like statements about human nature, and it follows from the doctrine of creation that he who made us knows better than anyone else what is good for us.

The headmaster might say: 'I forbid you to walk on that piece of grass, and if you disobey me often enough I will probably beat you.' God's laws are more like saying: 'If you jump from too great a height you will probably come to grief because the universe has to be so ordained that gravity exists.'

To translate this into moral laws we might take, for instance, monogamy. This is sometimes treated as an extension of the principle of fair shares. There are not quite the same number of men and women in the world, but neither sex outnumbers the other sufficiently to permit of more than one partner in life each.

But I would take the issue deeper than this and find the answer in human nature, which would mean the principle that men and women are so constituted as to find their deepest fulfilment in a life-long partnership with one person. If this is true, the moral requirement of monogamy is more like the application of the law of gravity than the prohibition to walk on the grass. If Christian moral standards merely reflect the deepest truths about human nature, it would seem in the interests of mankind that they should be everywhere imposed.

But you may be thinking of cases where the keeping of God's laws seems to be impossible without that grace which is the special concomitant of faith. There are those who have made poverty or chastity their rule, and have triumphed because the love of God has been so strong in their lives as to enable them to avoid embitterment. For without such an irradiation of Divine love these loads can be too heavy for people to bear, and we must remember our Lord's condemnation of the Pharisees for precisely this sort of overloading.

We must, I think, distinguish between the basic moral standards which apply to all and the call to heroic sacrifice which is to the individual and which, if it *is* a call, will be accompanied by a grace which is sufficient for the purpose.

RIGHT & WRONG

'Why does mankind find the terms "right" and "wrong" so difficult to define?'

I WOULD alter your question to 'Why do we find it so difficult to agree on a definition?' - there are definitions in plenty. I fully recognize the truth of the attitude implied by your question, but it does not do to overstress the differences of opinion. The considerable overlap of agreement is important also.

I note in many of the arguments of the humanist an insistence on the fact that it is possible to *be* good without having a belief in God. I rather think they are sticking to safe ground here, since the fact is incontrovertible. They seem less anxious to venture out into the question of how the quality of goodness is defined.

If mankind did in fact agree more completely on the answer, their position would be stronger. But the argument which I have heard often, 'All right-minded people agree ...' merely pushes the question back to how you define 'right'-mindedness.

I find a lot of help from looking at the non-ethical use of the terms 'good' and 'bad'. They can usually be rephrased as 'fulfils its purpose effectively' and 'does not fulfil its purpose effectively'. A 'good' instrument of torture is one which gets the victim talking.

It is at least worth seeing if this has not some light to shed on how we might identify, for instance, a 'good' man. It would require the assumption that man is made for a purpose – and this, to my way of thinking, implies that man has a maker and that this maker has the quality of mind. I cannot picture purpose as being possible except as the creation of a mind.

A *good* man, in Christian terms, would thus be a man who is fulfilling effectively the purpose for which God created him. A *good* action would be one that helped him along the road to that destination. If you have no intended destination you cannot properly ask, 'Am I on the *right* road?' This may be very satisfactory as a theory, but it cannot work out in practice unless we know what the destination is or the purpose for which we were created.

There are two possible solutions. One is that God has marked out the course – that all the wrong turnings are marked in advance, 'No Entry.' I always remember the Cornishman, of whom I had asked the way, saying: 'Ye know Trevarrian? Ye don't go there.'

The other possible solution is that the road is not marked out, or at least not fully signposted, but that we are given a guide. 'If ye are led of the Spirit, ye are not under the Law.' It was, I think, William Temple who described the moral life as an adventure. If this is true, it is more important to 'walk daily with God' than to be able to define right and wrong.

IS SUICIDE WRONG?

*'Does the Church of England have anything to say about
the rightness or wrongness of taking one's life?'*

THE QUESTION would be easier to answer if it were
possible to make a clear distinction between self-destruction
and self-sacrifice.

In the history of Christian thought it has been usual to
condemn the act *and* to allow for certain 'honourable
exceptions'. I think that this reflects the distinction. One
of the difficulties has been that, once suicide is allowed a
place among the heinous offences, it quickly rises to the
top of the list because the possibility of repentance is,
almost by definition, excluded. Hence the severity of some
Christian judgements.

So far as the Church of England is concerned, there was
a report entitled *Ought Suicide to be a Crime?* produced for
the Board for Social Responsibility in 1959 by a committee
under the chairmanship of John Christie, then Principal of
Jesus College, Oxford. Their recommendation that suicide
should cease to be a legal offence does not preclude the
possibility of its remaining a moral offence.

Under this heading they listed various categories of
suicide, of which two were specifically excluded from
censure: 'those which are involuntary - insofar as they are
done under external compulsion (such as torture or the
threat of rape)' and those where mental derangement can be
asserted.

Their next category is those which are 'voluntary but
altruistic'. These include acts of self-sacrifice and
self-euthanasia. It is here that we need to focus our
attention; the fourth category - 'voluntary and selfish' -
seems by definition to be wrong.

Most of the traditional arguments would condemn even
the altruistic suicides. They tend to rely on the assertion
that 'God alone should prescribe the end of a man's life.'
David Hume argued convincingly that this principle would
also condemn every form of life-saving, medical or
otherwise. It seems to me also to entail the condemnation of
all forms of homicide, capital punishment and euthanasia
included. Its exponents are not always consistent.

In deciding whether an act of suicide is self-destruction
or self-sacrifice, we are looking back from the act to the
motive which prompted it. The only ground on which the

traditional 'honourable exceptions' could be justified would be by the principle that, if we applaud the motive, we approve the act.

'KILL' OR 'MURDER'?

'Should we prefer "Thou shalt not kill" to "Thou shalt do no murder"?'

THE QUESTION raises, in a very interesting way, the more fundamental question whether it is the duty of a translator of the Bible to keep close to his text or to indulge in a certain measure of interpretation.

The word 'murder' is one of those which condemn an action without defining it. I would define murder as 'deliberate and unjustifiable homicide.' If you accept that, you would have to go outside the word itself to discover what circumstances rendered homicide justifiable. The *Oxford English Dictionary* uses the term 'unlawful.' If you prefer that, you would have to go to the statute-books to discover what forms of homicide are proscribed by the law of the land. These definitions are going to vary somewhat under different civilizations and at different times. 'Murder' was an offence at Auschwitz. There is therefore a *prima facie* case against the translation 'murder.'

The Hebrew word *ratsach*, which is used in both Exodus and Deuteronomy for the Sixth Commandment, is one of twelve different words which are sometimes translated 'kill' in the Old Testament. It covers a wider ground than 'murder' in English, in that it can include killing that is not deliberate. Unfortunately it only occurs on three other occasions in the Old Testament, with the result that we have little guidance on what might be its particular shade of meaning in the Decalogue.

This might seem to be argument in favour of 'Thou shalt not kill', were this not subject to the severe disadvantage of being contradicted by certain other texts. In Leviticus 20:16 the command, 'Thou shalt kill', appears in connection with a woman convicted of bestiality. In fact the words 'thou shalt kill' or 'ye shall kill' occur on quite a number of occasions, but never translating *ratsach*.

It is here, where words seem to have failed us, that we need to get on to interpretation. What did the words mean to those who used them? Undoubtedly those to whom the

Ten Commandments were first sacred did not so interpret *ratsach* as to preclude the taking of human life in war or in capital punishment. The command, 'Thou shalt kill', is usually applied in this latter context. Historically, the Church has usually agreed with this interpretation.

But I have so often heard 'Thou shalt not kill' invoked as an argument against war or against hanging – which is not, in the light of what I have just said, a legitimate argument – that I tend to favour 'Thou shalt do no murder' as at least avoiding this obvious misunderstanding.

WILLINGNESS TO FORGIVE

'"To understand all is to forgive all." Is this consistent with Christian teaching?'

I CANNOT quite place your quotation; it seems to come more naturally in French: 'tout comprendre c'est tout pardonner.' I wonder if this is not just an epigrammatic form of Mme de Staël's more cautious maxim, 'tout comprendre rend très indulgent,' which I would render: 'a full understanding makes us very ready to forgive.' Not such a neat epigram, but perhaps more strictly true. We should beware of epigrams.

Obviously we have to consider the different shades of meaning in the word 'forgive'. It can mean to remit a punishment; it can mean not to hold it against a person; or it can have its full Christian content of resuming the relationship of love which was broken by the sin – as illustrated by the parable of the Prodigal Son.

I think that it is the second of these meanings which fits Mme de Staël's maxim. It is closely connected with the question of blame. It is quite possible to condemn a person's action, and then to take such a view of that person's heredity and environment as to acquit him of any blame.

But full Christian forgiveness, which is virtually the same as reconciliation, is a two-way process requiring a move on both sides. 'If he repent, forgive him.' If he will not repent, you can only reach the stage, unilaterally, of being ready to forgive or of not holding it against the person.

One of the most impressive opinions on this subject is that of Laurens van der Post in his book, *The Night of the*

New Moon. It could almost be called an essay in forgiveness. In the first place he had more than most of us will ever have to forgive. He is entitled to a hearing.

He speaks of the atrocities of the Japanese and of the underlying reasons for their brutality, which, in his own words, 'made it impossible for people like ourselves, even at our worst moments in prison, to have any personal feelings against our captors, because it made us realize how the Japanese were themselves the puppets of immense impersonal forces to such an extent that they did not know what they were doing.'

Even more relevant to the present issue is his account of his many fellow-prisoners who had, in this act of understanding, for the first time in their lives 'realized the truth and the dynamic liberating power of the first of the Crucifixion utterances: 'Forgive them, for they know not what they do.'

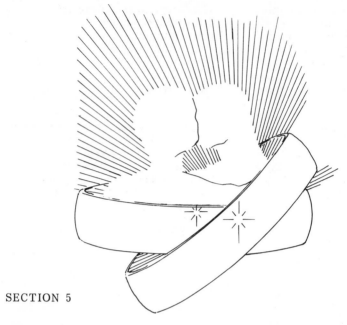

SECTION 5

Sex

CHARITY & CHASTITY

'Should a Christian think charity more important than chastity?'

YES. The whole is always more important than the part. Look at the 13th chapter of I Corinthians: 'though I bestow all my goods to feed the poor and give my body to be burned and have not charity, it profiteth me nothing.' You could add to that: 'though I observe the strictest chastity and have not charity, I am nothing.'

I think that the question only arises because of our debasement of the word 'charity'. It *can* mean flipping sixpence to a beggar. It *should* mean really caring about people.

If you really care for people, you would not exploit them for your pleasure or profit. That rules out some forms of unchastity straight off. But it is no good condemning unchastity on this count and turning a blind eye to the other forms of exploitation. There has been a tendency on the part of Churchpeople to do this, and we are paying for it heavily today.

If you really care about people, you would desire only the highest and the best for them; and it is a point of Christian teaching and experience that the highest and best use of sex is when it is unique to the marriage relationship – when two people can feel: 'this is something that *we* share which we have never shared with anyone else.' It is no charity to deprive someone of the opportunity of this unique relationship.

But I want to make another point here. It is no charity to deprive yourself of it either. We are told to love our neighbours *as ourselves*. This becomes somewhat meaningless if we do not really love ourselves – if we do not really care about the sort of persons we are becoming. Really caring about yourself is part of Christian living.

When our Lord said that all moral laws depended on the Law of Love, I believe that he was saying that love is the source from which all actions derive their virtue. If they are not tinged with that, they are not virtues. Chastity that does not derive from love is a mean and withered plant in which it is difficult to recognize any virtue at all.

Chastity is not popular today – perhaps because it has been too often seen divorced from love. It is a healthy corrective to read the eulogy of it in Milton's *Comus: 'So dear to Heaven is saintly chastity.'*

EQUATING SEX WITH 'DIRT'

'I wonder if you are right in your condemnation of the Church's "equation of sex with dirt". Have you any proof that any such equation was ever made? There are too many attempts these days to undermine the Church's traditional teaching.'

BERTRAND RUSSELL, in his book *Marriage & Morals* (1929), said that the task of the reformer was 'to cleanse sex from the filth with which it has been covered by

Christian moralists'.

Even if no one was actually teaching that sex was something filthy, it was certainly thought in high intellectual circles that such teaching was being given. As a great deal of the teaching of the Church is done by word of mouth - in preaching, in counselling and in the confessional - there is obviously nothing like a complete record. But the climate of opinion is usually clear enough.

I have certainly read of a Headmaster of Eton (I think it was Warre) who gave a talk to new boys in which he referred to 'filth' - and by 'filth' they took him to mean sex. I am afraid I cannot supply chapter and verse.

A vicar once told me that he had admitted to Communion an unmarried mother, having carefully satisfied himself that it was the right thing to do. After the service another woman came up and expressed her disgust and disapproval, and refused to come to the altar-rail with a 'sinner'.

The vicar very rightly pointed out that '*all* have sinned and fallen short of the glory of God', that he himself had committed many sins and so had the woman to whom he was talking. At this she drew herself up in righteous indignation and said: 'not THAT'. I suspect that she was not untypical.

To many people the very term 'Christian morality' is likely to suggest immediately a negative attitude towards sex, as if this were the *great offence*. Many who will cheerfully ignore the Bible's teaching on pride, covetousness, snobbery, litigation, almsgiving and forgiving 'unto seventy times seven' suddenly become fundamentalists and legalists when they find a reference to fornication or homosexuality.

As to my 'undermining' the Church's traditional teaching, I would rather say that I was rejecting it as a misrepresentation of the truth. The Church's traditional teaching has been frequently off balance, out of proportion if not downright wrong. It has often failed to give proper weight to the doctrine of Creation (once again see I Timothy 4:4) and to the supremacy of love in Christian ethical teaching.

N.B. I do not know of any book which sets forth as authoritative what I here call the Church's 'traditional teaching'. I have found much help in Douglas Rhymes' No New Morality (1964).

FORNICATION – A 'DEADLY SIN'?

'In the Litany fornication is referred to as "deadly sin".
Does the Church offer any corporate teaching on this
matter? Is it at variance with the Biblical teaching?'

I WOULD like to start with the more cautious statement that
the New Testament undoubtedly condemns *porneia*.

You quote in your list of Bible references I Corinthians
6:13. I hope you read on a few verses: 'Shall I take the
members of Christ and make them members of a harlot?' The
Greek for harlot is *pornee*. The proper meaning, then of
porneia is to have recourse to a harlot; and, in this
passage at least, it must be taken in this sense.

Notice also the association between *porneia* and idolatry.
The harlot was very often one of the 'holy women' who were
religious prositutes. Condemnations of *porneia* are probably
more often concerned to forbid taking part in the worship
of a false god than with what we mean today by sexual
ethics.

I do not say that every reference in the New Testament
has to be taken in this sense. The word can also mean
sexual depravity in a general and undefined way. But it is
equally true that in no case does the word necessarily mean
'sex before marriage'.

The Church, however, has not on the whole argued in
this way. It has throughout the ages regarded sex outside
marriage as a sin. How you interpret this will depend upon
your overall view of the basis of ethics.

There are those (and they include the majority of
Churchpeople) who believe that certain actions can be
labelled 'right' or 'wrong', just as certain objects can be
labelled 'red' or 'blue'. St Paul, in the famous passage in I
Corinthians 13, makes it quite clear that this is not what he
regards as the Christian system. He sees moral value
entirely in terms of the presence or absence of love.

Sex without love, therefore – which would include
prostitution as understood today – is clearly condemned.
But, if rightness and wrongness are not regarded as
inherent in an action, there is room for further argument.
Fornication could be wrong only because it is liable to
produce an illegitimate child. The teaching of the Church
against fornication was evolved in an age when reliable
contraceptives were not available. The only way to ensure
that no child was born out of wedlock was to forbid sex

outside wedlock.

These arguments are not unreasonable nor unscriptural. I do not myself regard them as decisive. I think that the highest and the best use of sex is when it is unique to the marriage relationship, and that anything which falls short of the highest and the best is sin.

CHRISTIANS & SEX

'Do Anglicans welcome the Pope's negative attitude on sexual ethics?'

I CAN only speak for myself. My guess is that, whereas such a pronouncement will be like a drink of water in a thirsty land to those who already agree with its conclusions, it will fall, as it has usually fallen, on largely deaf ears so far as the great majority are concerned.

Anyone of my age has had plenty of opportunity of judging the effects of a sexual morality based on those prohibitions. I grew up in the climate of opinion which they had created. My own father was never able to mention sex to me at all. My mother tried to, but she approached the subject as a parabolic curve approaches a straight line; we never really got there.

My school, where the subject was classified as *General Biology 'A'*, offered a rather tedious film on the copulation of frogs. When I reached puberty, what I didn't know about the sex life of the Natterjack Toad simply wasn't worth knowing. What I did know wasn't worth knowing either. It was a singularly useless raft on which to navigate the troubled waters of adolescence.

One of my schoolmasters, to be fair, did offer the help I needed, but by then I was too inhibited to avail myself of the offer. He was, as it happens, a clergyman, but I would not have dreamed at that age of looking to the Church for guidance. I was not interested in negative attitudes.

Long ago I remember a letter in the *Church Times* in which a married woman described sex *within* marriage as 'a few seconds selfish pleasure' on the part of the man. Poor woman! And poor man! In this context I would like to say how much I regret the replacement of the words 'with my body *I thee worship*' by '*I thee honour*' in the marriage service. The old Prayer Book sometimes wins.

Not quite so long ago someone used the term 'holy

communion' to describe sex (as Dr Eric Abbott then said: 'Notice the small "h" and the small "c"'), and I remember the outcry. Whatever we may think of that comparison, it is a fact that the basic meaning of holy is 'set apart'. With a capital 'H' it means 'set apart for God'.

I believe as deeply as I believe anything that marriage is holy - 'keep thee only unto him/her as long as you both shall live.' It is a relationship - and I speak simply from experience - set apart from all other relationships. I believe also that sex is God's special gift to that relationship and constitutes what is essentially unique about it. Like everything created by God it is good 'if it is received with thanksgiving'. The Greek is of course *eucharistia*, and gives the idea of consecrating by thanksgiving.

This exalted peak of communion in human relationship is the target. Anything that falls short of the target set by God is by definition sin. But let us not forget that we believe in the forgiveness of sins.

SEX DIVORCED FROM EROS

'You always seem hostile to those who are trying to maintain the traditional Christian position on sex'.

MY POINT is that this position is often too negative. I do not mean that there are no times when it is necessary to tell people that their actions are wrong. But it is ultimately harmful if you never build up the picture of what is right.

I keep emphasizing in this column that Christian ethics are not really concerned with 'right' and 'wrong'. These words are not biblical. Our typical words are 'love' and 'sin'. Sin means 'falling short of the target'. It would be pretty silly to go on telling someone that he was failing to hit the target if you have never made it clear to him what that target is. That is what I mean by being positive, and that is where I believe the Church has largely failed in its traditional teaching.

If we are going to state that certain actions are wrong, it must always be against a background of what is right. And we need to be keenly perceptive of where the true locus of evil lies.

One answer to the question, 'What is wrong with the modern attitude to sex?', could be that we have allowed sex to be divorced from Eros. Socrates described Eros as being 'a great god (daimon) and, like all spirits, he is intermediate between the divine and the mortal ... he is the mediator who spans the chasm which divides men and gods.' Eros is the power that magnetizes the scholar to the truth, the artist to his vision. In human relationships Eros is the longing to establish true union and full relationship.

Rollo May identifies the position thus: 'The Victorian person sought to have love without falling into sex; the modern person seeks to have sex without falling into love'. He quotes Harvey Cox who calls *Playboy* 'the latest, slickest episode in man's refusal to be human'.

I believe that the root of today's ills is apathy, which is in many ways the opposite of Eros. Oddly, apathy breeds violence. To return to Rollo May: 'violence is the ultimate destructive subsitute which surges in to fill the vacuum where there is no relatedness'.

If we put sex firmly in its context of relatedness - as something which expresses, enriches and nourishes that tremendous desire for union which is typical of Eros - we not only enrich Eros; we enrich sex. What May condemns is the modern *banalisation* of sex.

SEXUAL VERSUS SOCIAL MORALITY

'If Christians stopped fussing about sex and attended to the real problems of world suffering, the Church might get more support.'

I WONDER if you are suggesting here that sex is not a 'real problem'? You remind me of an incident in a railway carriage in 1940, when a soldier lit up a cigarette in a non-smoker. An asthmatic old lady requested him to put it out and got the reaction, all too common in those days, 'Do you know there's a war on?' At this a man in the corner lowered his newspaper and answered for her: 'Yes - and, if our soldiers do not know what it is to obey regulations, we will lose it.' I was only fifteen at that time, but I was so impressed that I have remembered it ever since.

I am not favourably impressed by some of the methods of arguing employed by those who stand up for the permissive attitude to sex. One of their ruses is precisely to say 'keep off this ground; the real battle is not here'. I would rather hear them boldly answer with a defence of their position than to be thus evasive.

It is no doubt convenient for such people to assume also that the Church is unconcerned for the major problems of world suffering. This is not entirely true, as any regular reader of the *Church Times* must know.

But, however inadequate the Church's concern for world suffering and however widespread its interest in sex, it is absurd to argue that these two areas are somehow mutually exclusive. It is perfectly possible, and wholly desirable, that the Church should be involved in both.

Only somebody deeply ignorant of sex could possibly suggest that this was an aspect of life which anybody - or any organization involved in human welfare - could ever afford to ignore. There is a passage in Schopenhauer which I think deserves to be quoted at some length.

'Sexual passion is the cause of war and the end of peace, the basis of what is serious and the aim of the jest, the inexhaustible source of wit, the key to all allusions, and the meaning of all mysterious hints ... just because the profoundest seriousness lies at its foundation. ... But all this agrees with the fact that the sexual passion is the kernel of the will to live, and consequently the concentration of all desire.'

I quote this from Dr Rollo May's book, *Love and Will*, which I warmly recommend to those who uphold the permissive standards as well as to those churchmen whose upbringing has led them into a narrow and negative attitude which has brought upon them the wrath of people such as yourself.

MEANING OF CHASTITY

'Does chastity mean the "Christian use of sex", or abstinence from sex in all its forms?'

I AM afraid this question cannot be answered. Words mean what people use them to mean, and their meanings vary according to their context. It is often interesting to study their etymology, but it is equally often pedantic to insist upon the original meaning.

The monk or nun who took the vow of poverty, chastity and obedience undoubtedly thereby embraced celibacy. Ambrose, however, specifically commends chastity (for women) in three contexts - virginity, marriage and widowhood. At the Council of Nicaea a deputy named Paphnutius successfully defended ligitimate sexual intercourse within marriage as being within the definition of chastity.

The fact is that 'the Christian use of sex' is not a sufficiently precise definition. There has been a wide variety of opinion and widespread disagreement.

St Paul laid down the principle that it was better to marry than to burn. Eustochium, according to Jerome, felt it more meritorious to burn. He lived as a cenobite in the desert, inflicting every imaginable severity upon himself. 'My face was pale with fasting and my mind within my frigid body was burning with desire; the fires of lust would still flare up in a body which already seemed to be dead.' Although my heart goes out to the poor little man, I cannot help thinking that he was going about the wrong thing in the wrong way.

Another questionable practice of the early Church was that of sexless marriage. Chrysostom has some perspicacious remarks to make about the system, claiming that, since 'the gratification of desire never extinguishes the bright flame,' it therefore 'ever continues to increase in strength.'

Well, well. Some may prefer the sweeter pangs of unrequited love. There is no accounting for taste; but, if this was chastity, it seems to me to have been chastity of an uncommonly erotic nature.

The mistake which so many Christians seem to have made is to attempt the repression of the body without having first won the battle of the mind. In speaking of adultery our Lord took the centre of gravity out of the carnal act and placed it firmly in the mind that could look on a woman to lust after her. We have not sufficiently heeded his words.

I am in fact arguing for the use of the word 'chastity' to describe the state of mind of someone, whether married or not, who can contemplate the sexuality of others without lasciviousness.

N.B. *For further reading on this subject I recommend* Sherwin Bailey: The Man Woman Relationship in Christian Thought (1959) *and* Commonsense about Sexual Ethics. A Christian View (1962)

THE DEFINITION OF SEXUAL

*'Although Margaret Duggan claims to uphold the Christian
ideal of lifelong monogamy, surely her article, "Do we take
monogamy too far", is a threat to Christian morality?'*

THE CENTRE of gravity in Margaret Duggan's article is in
the sentence 'unfrightened and loving people ought to be
able to manage affectionate friendships which are admittedly
sexual but not necessarily genital.' I wonder if the
inversion of two words would not be all that you require.
For *not necessarily genital* read *necessarily not genital*.

But I would like to ask Margaret Duggan to spell out
more clearly what is meant by 'admittedly sexual'. I am not
sufficiently educated to read Freud with understanding.
Concepts such as 'de-sexualized libido' ring no bells within
me. But I do read and think I understand the American
psychiatrist Rollo May. 'Freud,' he writes in *Love and Will*,
sought to enrich and extend the concept of sex to include
everything from fondling and nursing to creativity and
religion.

'We use the word *sexuality* (he is quoting Morgan) in the
same comprehensive sense as that in which the German
language uses the word *lieben*.' To an amateur like myself
the German word lieben means Love.

If a Freudian tells me that *in this sense of the term* my
relations with my own children are 'sexual' I am not
dismayed, for I do not start with any basic idea that sex is
undesirable. But I may be confused. We come here to what
is not a question of truth, or of psychology, or of
morality, but a question of vocabulary. I would ask if it is
helpful in common parlance to use the term *sexual* of a
relationship which, according to my emendment of Mrs
Duggan's phrase, is necessarily not genital? And at the
same time I would ask the question: given the immensely
wide and comprehensive nature of the marital relationship,
is it appropriate to describe it by the very narrow term
genital?

Granted that the other affectionate relationships are, in
some sense, tinged with sex, is this not a different sort of
sexuality from that which characterizes the marital
relationship? The fondling and nursing of one's children
seem to me to take one down a *different* road from the
physical caresses of husband and wife, rather than down
the same road with a 'thus-far-but-no-further' notice before

we reach the stage qualified as genital.

I would myself prefer, simply as a matter of useful vocabulary, the retention of the word 'sexual' for the road which desires to end in the genital, and to use some other term for what Mrs Duggan calls the 'non-genital affectionate friendships'. I am all in favour of these, especially among Christians, but I really could not seriously use that term.

PUTTING SEX IN ITS PLACE

'I am quite bewildered by contradictory attitudes of Church-men to sex. Is there such a thing as a Christian standard?'

IF YOU look no deeper than the surface manifestations of the problem today, you probably are bewildered. Christians denouncing the Dean of St Paul's for inviting the cast of *Hair* to Holy Communion; Christians denouncing the denouncers. Where in this whirlpool is the truth to be found?

To me one of the more sinister aspects of it all is the centrifugal force which appears to be driving people more and more towards extreme positions. Here, more than anywhere, we need the steadying influence of the dictum of Boileau - 'La parfaite raison fuit toute extrémité' (The perfect reason recoils from all extremes). The truth, as ever, is in the middle.

It would seem to me to be not unreasonable to go for an answer to Jesus Christ himself. If we were to tabulate his teaching topic by topic so as to produce a chart showing, as thermometer readings, the amount of teaching which he gave on each, we would find by far the tallest column (and therefore the greatest area of concern) representing the sins of pharisaism - that is to say legalism, with its ugly concomitants of self-righteousness, vindictiveness and hypocrisy. The reading on the sex thermometer would be quite small.

So immediately we find the problem cut down to size. This is not the centre of gravity of Christian ethics. As Joseph Fletcher put it: 'It is not sexual behaviour that determines character - it is character that determines sexual behaviour.'

If we then pass to an evaluation of such teaching as Jesus did give on the subject, we will find the longest and most explicit passage is the story of the Woman taken in

Adultery. Jesus does not hesitate to call her action a sin, but he at once diverts attention away from it to the sins of those who wanted to penalize her. If this had been the charter of the Church throughout the ages, we should not be in the mess which we see today.

Jesus' general attitude towards such sinners as harlots was one of love and readiness to forgive. It is more typical of Churchmen to refuse to have 'that sort of woman' in the house.

In the main both Protestants and Catholics have been pharisaic in their attitudes to sex. Even its legitimate use has often been at best a grudging concession. Jerome would only countenance it as an unfortunate prerequisite to the procreation of future virgins!

To end on a positive note, I would merely remind you that *everything*, including sex, *created by God is good and nothing to be refused if it be taken with thanksgiving*; but I would regard it as inconsistent with such gratitude to debase God's gift into a cheap form of entertainment. Sex and love should not be set asunder.

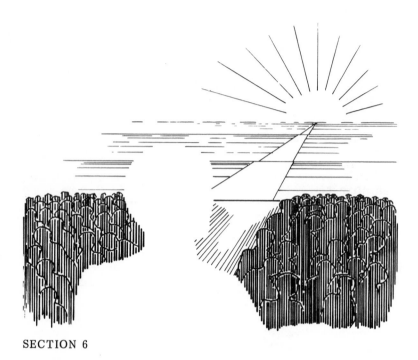

Faith

A SIMPLE, TRUSTING FAITH

'What did Jesus mean by saying that, unless we are converted and become as little children, we shall not enter into the Kingdom of Heaven?'

I WOULD not myself have the presumption to lay down the law about *what* Christ *meant* by words which allow of a variety of interpretation. It seems to me that much of what he said was of an enigmatic nature, and that we miss the point if we seek a hard-and-fast definition.

Cranmer has a splendid phrase somewhere that in the Scriptures we find 'the fat pastures of the soul'. It is full of overtones of the process of intake, rumination, digestion and finally receiving nourishment. Another useful metaphor

is to regard Scripture as the *seminal* word. The ideas of
food for thought and of a seed planted in the mind lie close
to one another.

I can only tell you what my own ruminations on this
passage have produced. The relevant quality that I see in
children is a sort of openness towards the future – a
delight in discovering new things – an eagerness about the
huge, unfolding panorama of life. To see a child's eyes
dancing with excitement as he stands on the threshold of
some new experience is often to experience a sharp pang as
we realize that we have grown old and dull.

And yet I have seen that look on the face of a very old
woman. She was one of the few people with whom I have
been able to talk without any embarrassment about her
death. Her eyes would light up with excitement. There was
no arrogance in her assumption that Heaven was her
destiny: just a simple trust that Jesus Christ would see her
through. Not many Christians in old age have enough faith
to breed hope. When I was talking to this woman I felt I
knew what our Lord meant about becoming like children.

I think he was trying to counter the stodgy,
security-seeking, self-satisfaction of middle age. My mind
flits to a man in his middle fifties to whom every new idea
was a threat. His commonest phrases were 'what I was
always taught' and 'what we've always done'. His
perspective of life was always back into the past. He had
been taught – Heaven knows how – to receive Communion
once a year and to dig his garden on Good Friday. No
earthly power would have got him to budge from that.
Somebody, at some time, somehow pushed that one idea into
the tube, where it stuck and for ever blocks the passage.

Wordsworth, to me, has the last word on the subject in
his 'Ode on Intimations of Immortality':

> *Heaven lies about us in our infancy!*
> *Shades of the prison-house begin to close*
> *Upon the growing boy,*
> *But he beholds the light, and whence it flows*
> *He sees it in his joy;*
> *The youth, who daily farther from the east*
> *Must travel, still is nature's priest,*
> *And by the vision splendid*
> *   Is on his way attended;*
> *At length the man perceives it die away,*
> *And fade into the light of common day.*

GOODNESS OF CREATION

'If you take seriously the sinfulness of man, is it possible to believe that God's creation is good?'

'GOD created man in his own image and likeness,' wrote Berdayaev in *The Destiny of Man* – 'i.e., he made him a creator too, calling him to free spontaneous activity and not to a formal obedience to his power. Free creativeness is the creature's answer to the great call of its creator.'

I wonder if you are not wishing that God had made a puppet world in which his will was invariably obeyed. At first sight such a creation might well appear to be 'good'. Nobody would be doing anything 'bad'. But in fact a puppet is a morally neutral thing. It cannot be either good or bad. If it is made to perform the part of a saint, it does not become thereby capable of saintliness; if it is cast as a villain, it is not itself capable of villainy.

There is a most interesting theory in Dorothy L. Sayers' *The Mind of the Maker*, in the chapter entitled 'Free Will and Miracle', in which she discusses the creation of a character by a playwright. 'It appears obvious,' she says, 'that the characters invented by a human writer are his helpless puppets, bound to obey his will at every point whether for good or for evil.'

But, if you ask why it is that some characters in fiction or drama are entirely dull and unconvincing, whereas others are vital and ring true, you get deeper into the problem. At this level Miss Sayers detects a kind of autonomy in a character of fiction; 'unless the author permits them to develop in conformity with their proper nature, they will cease to be true and living creatures.'

Miss Sayers also makes use of the simile of parenthood. Although the parent is wholly responsible for calling the child into being, nevertheless the child has a capacity for independence which it is the proper function of the parent to respect and to nourish. The worst type of parent is that which tries to keep its offspring in total dependence, and in total conformity with his or her mind.

If we mean anything by calling God 'Father' we mean that our own experience of parenthood – at its best – can give us an insight into the nature of God. If earthly parents can give their children that precious independence, how much more will our Heavenly Father do so? It is only when a creature rises to the level of making a free return of the love which issued in its creation that the word 'good' can properly be used.

THROUGH A GLASS DARKLY

'Do you not think that the adulation bestowed by some upon royalty ought to be reserved for God?'

I WONDER if the same question might not be asked of a child's love for its mother. Should this love not be reserved for God?

There are two different ways of relating this world to the next. One is by setting them in opposition to one another; the other is by setting them in sequence.

Those who take the former view mistrust any experience that is enjoyable for fear that it should attach them to this world and prevent them from pressing on to the next. Those who take the second view see in their experience of this world intimations of the next. They find in earthly love the nearest thing to divine love and a necessary stepping stone to it.

I would like to be able to illustrate my point by taking the words of the Authorised Version, 'here we see through a glass darkly, but then face to face.' Alas, it is a very poor translation. The Greek says *in a mirror*, not *through a glass*, and *in enigmas*, not *darkly*.

Nevertheless, the idea of a person looking through smoked glass at the sun, and then being dazzled by the same sun, does fit St Paul's general theme of an experience which is partial in this world and total in the next. The two are in suite with each other and not in competition.

If this is the correct view of the relationship of the two worlds, then I can see no reason for being suspicious of loyalty to an earthly Sovereign. It could and should merely be preparing your heart for loyalty to the Heavenly King – just as I would argue that love for a human parent (or, indeed, for any human being) opens our hearts to the possibility of loving our Heavenly Father. 'He that loveth not his brother whom he hath seen, how can he love God whom he hath not seen?' That seems to me to settle the matter.

I do not wish to imply, however, that the progress from one level to the next is automatic. We can always remain contented with our earthly experience and fail to see it as a pointer to something beyond it.

FRUIT OF THE SPIRIT

'Evelyn Underhill quotes Madeleine Semer as saying: "I was seized, possessed by an internal flame ... waves of fire succeeding each other for some two hours." What ground have we for believing that this kind of experience is a touch of God or a manifestation of the Holy Spirit?'

WE ARE in no position to judge the religious experience of other people. If God chooses to make his presence felt to some people in an experience of inner warmth, so be it. Richard Rolle also claimed an 'unwonted and pleasant heat' burning his soul. Such experiences may sometimes accompany a life lived near to God.

But I do not think that you can ever argue *from* the experience *to* God, and I think that there can be real danger in hankering after some such experience. It is always dangerous to divert your attention from the real thing to the pleasing sensation attendant upon the real thing.

We are warned of the possibility of false spirits (I John 4:1), and we must therefore not assume that anything identified as a manifestation of spirit is necessarily the Holy Spirit. This is where the authority of Scripture comes in. If that is accepted, the picture of the Holy Spirit afforded by the New Testament becomes authentic, and every experience of spirit must be tested against it.

There is a list of the 'fruit of the Spirit' given in Galatians 5:22 – 'love, joy, peace, longsuffering, gentleness, goodness, faith, meekness, temperance (I would prefer the translation 'self-control' to *temperance*, which is too often connected in people's minds with abstinence from alcohol). If the spirit which manifests itself in some 'religious' experience is also producing the typical fruit of the Spirit, you may feel confidence that this is no false spirit.

Of all that list, the only item that looks like being an emotional experience is joy. I have always identified joy with the feeling, *this is what I was made for*. It is as if God had laid down a path in life for me and every now and then, amid my erring and straying, my actual path coincides with his ordained path. Everything suddenly seems to be as it was meant to be.

But it is no use hankering after joy. It only comes to those who tread that path.

BELIEF IN MIRACLES

'Is it necessary to believe in miracles in order to believe in Christianity?'

I SUPPOSE it depends to some extent on what you mean by *miracles*, but I certainly do not go along with those whose fundamental position is to think that 'no honest intellectual could accept the idea of a miracle these days, so we must find some other explanation for these stories.'

My own position as a Christian owes a great deal to C.S. Lewis. It was his writings that won me from adolescent scepticism about the 'fairy story' religion in which I was brought up. And he most emphatically believed in the reality of the supernatural and in the ability of the supernatural to penetrate this world order. I have never myself seen anything 'dishonest' or even 'unintellectual' in C.S. Lewis.

One of his more important books is entitled *Miracles*; and I quote from this his belief 'that, in addition to the physical or psycho-physical universe known to the sciences, there exists an uncreated and unconditioned reality which causes the universe to be'; and that 'this reality at a definite point in time entered the universe we know by becoming one of its own creatures, and there produced effects on the historical level which the normal workings of the natural universe do not produce.'

With typical awareness of the quality of language, Lewis adds: 'It will be noticed that our colourless "entered the universe" is not a whit less metaphorical than the more picturesque "came down from Heaven" ... We can make speech duller; we cannot make it more literal.'

But, while Lewis defends what you might call the 'central miracle' of the Incarnation by insisting on the necessity of metaphor, he equally insists that it is necessary to treat the subsequent miracles literally. The turning of water into wine, for instance, 'refers to something which, if it happened, was well within the reach of our senses and our language.'

I have no space here to elaborate his argument, and can

only refer you to the book of *Miracles* itself. It is written
with an admirable lucidity, and you will learn a lot about
the use of language and the method of argument as well as
about miracles themselves.

ANOTHER SORT OF 'PROPHECY'

*'It used to be complained that we never heard the prophetic
voice of the Church. We now seem to hear it to the exclusion
of all else,'*

THE WORD 'prophetic' is one with a very wide variety of
meanings. It seems to have become limited, in some circles,
to the drawing of attention to social evils. When people
complain of the absence of the 'prophetic voice of the
Church,' they usually mean that the Church is not
emulating Wilberforce and Shaftesbury in the nineteenth
century.

This is, of course, in line with the role of the Old
Testament prophets, and as such it has its place in the
Church's area of responsibility. But there is a very
different sense to the words 'prophet' and 'prophesy' in the
New Testament which I think we tend to neglect.

It is treated at some length in I Corinthians 14. In this
passage St Paul distinguishes between 'prophesying' and
'speaking with tongues'. The latter, translated in the New
English Bible as 'the language of ecstacy', is given a place
- perhaps rather a grudging place - by St Paul in a man's
private devotions: 'he speaks not to man but to God.' The
man who prophesies, however, speaks to men; and the
hallmarks of such prophesying are that they 'have power to
build; they stimulate and encourage (NEB)'.

'Power to build' or edification (AV) means, quite
literally, to build a house - but the word 'house' can be
understood as in the expression 'the House of Windsor',
meaning the family. To speak edifying words, then, is not
to provide moral uplift - which is its normal connotation
today - but to contribute to the sense of fellowship which
is so fundamental a part of the Church.

The second word is translated 'exhortation' in the
Authorised Version and 'to stimulate' in the NEB. Neither of
these seem to me quite adequate. It is in Greek the word
'paraclete' which is also used of the Holy Spirit. I always
feel that 'comforter' is a soft word, and ill-expresses what

it stands for here. The accent should be on the syllable *fort*. It means to fortify or strengthen; not something that invites you to relax but something that braces you for endurance.

I do not think that the third word, 'encouragement', really adds anything to the other two.

I think that there can be little doubt that this is the sort of 'prophecy' which is listed by St Paul in I Corinthians 12 among the charismatic gifts. It does not often seem to get a mention.

CALLED TO BE SAINTS

'I always feel that All Saints' Day merely shows up the unreality of Christian teaching about the saints.'

'PURITANICAL PEOPLE,' writes Helen Roeder, 'sometimes become indignant over those fabulous saints, but they have a profound significance. They are the nursery tales of the Church and they testify ... to the wonderful creative power which can take the old, deep things of human nature and consecrate them.'

She is quite honest in her book, *Saints and their Attributes*, about the naivety and credulity behind some of the Church's hagiology. I was particularly touched with her account of St Decimil, whose pathetic epitaph was the simple mention of his name. He was never officially canonised, but it was only after years of local devotions that it was realized that his tombstone was, in fact, a milestone.

Hardly less apocryphal was St Expeditus, 'the patron of prompt decisions'. He bears, in early Christian art, a suspicious resemblance to Mercury. I doubt if the most puritanical among us would reproach the Greeks for their mythological figures. They related to something deep in man's psychology, and it was part of the wisdom of the early Church to accept this mythology and to naturalize it into the Christian Faith.

The need to have a local worthy as a figure of respect and awe is surely understandable. I found what has proved, for me, the best expression of it in an obscure article in a learned periodical about the little church of St Arnoult-en-Yvlines between Chartres and Paris.

'There lies sleeping,' writes the Abbe Lechaugette, 'the member of the mystical body, already in glory, now finally united to the Head, bearing witness to every member of the living body in this place now on earth of their common faith, their common hope and their single love.' Let not sophistication hear, with a disdainful smile, the often childish aids to simple faith.

But there is another side to the matter. For a worshipper to derive inspiration from some local worthy is one thing; for the Church to claim the right to state who is in Heaven and the power to manipulate his intercessory assistance is another. It is a healthy corrective to remember that in the New Testament the word *saint* – with a small 's' – means an ordinary Christian such as you or me. The word means 'holy'; 'holy' means 'set apart' or 'devoted'.

All we need to know is that we are all 'called to be saints' – invited by the grace of God to be holy, even as he also is holy.

JESUS OF FAITH – AND HISTORY

'We have recently heard the opinion that there is no "hard evidence" for the existence of Jesus Christ. Would you please comment?'

IF YOU saw a monster in Loch Ness and had no camera and no other witness with you, your account of the experience might not be accepted as 'hard' evidence. Your words might carry *conviction* enough for a certain number to believe, on your testimony, that such a monster does exist. There would remain the sceptics who would claim that they still had no proof.

Christianity deals in terms of conviction rather than of proof. Proof would in fact destroy the element of faith. Conviction that Christ is a reality normally requires an element of personal experience, together with a backing of reason sufficient to create conviction.

I often wonder if those who remain determinedly sceptical about the value of the evidence that Jesus existed pay enough attention to the opposite conclusion, which is that the gospel narratives were deliberate invention.

It is one thing to cook up a story about an imaginary figure in some remote area at some not too clearly specified date. It is quite another to accuse the actual Roman Procurator and the actual High Priest, together with the members of his Sanhedrin, of executing this imaginary figure after a trial which was in many ways irregular and unjust. It is simply asking to be contradicted.

Both the Jewish and the Roman authorities had every reason to contradict it and, if truth were on their side, could have done so quite easily. There is no record that they did contradict it; and, if they did, it is not easy to account for the rapid spread of belief in Jesus Christ.

We might also ask if the documents *look* like a cooked-up story. We should be on the look-out for 'eye-witness' touches. Why, for instance, are the sons of Simon of Cyrene mentioned, by Mark, by name? They have no significance to the course of events. Matthew and Luke saw no reason for including them. It looks to me like a deliberate authenticating touch, as much as to say: 'Simon of Cyrene - you know, the father of Rufus and Alexander - if you don't believe me, ask *them*.'

It is also encouraging that the different accounts do not wholly agree with each other. Was there one man - or angel - at the empty tomb, or were there two? Did the two Marys go to the tomb alone, or were they accompanied by Salome or by Joanna? I can only say that, if I were cooking up a story, I would not let discrepancies of that sort creep in.

I am not offering 'hard evidence'. But this sort of consideration increases my conviction - born of personal experience - that, when the Gospels talk of Jesus and the events of his life and death, they are referring to a historical reality.

God

OUR IMAGE OF GOD

'Don't you think artists have done great damage to religion by representing God as an old man with a beard?'

YES. If I were prepared to represent God in human form at all, I would represent him as a young man.

The further back in history one goes, it seems, the more old age was held in reverence. It had, of course, a scarcity value which it does not possess today. The idea of the *sage* - the old man whose long experience of life is the foundation of his wisdom - can be evoked; but is that the sort of image that we want to create of God?

Old age, a commonplace today, is more likely to

introduce overtones of retirement and inactivity, even if not of decrepitude and being 'on the shelf'.

Also I would be extremely chary of setting up an identification between great age and eternity. I wish we could get rid of the word 'everlasting' from our liturgy. It is practically a swear-word, and it encourages this identification. Eternity is not a very, very long time: it is more like timelessness. As this is a concept we are hardly capable of formulating, no adequate images exist.

Obviously God is neither young nor old, but there is something to be got out of the idea of God as a young man - vigorous, active, creative, procreative. It picks up man's perennial hankering for eternal youth, which is a recurrent theme in folk myth. Mediaeval sculptors had a tradition of representing those who clambered out of their graves at the last trump as all being in the prime of life - the age of Jesus at *his* resurrection.

The idea also fits the image of God as *father*. The word 'father', of course, says nothing about a man's age; there are young fathers and old fathers. But, if we link this idea of father with the saying that we must become like children (and little children at that), it suggests a father in the prime of life.

But, having said all this, I must end with a warning that it is extremely dangerous to think of God for long in any sort of human form. Metaphors should not be pressed too far. Quick insights may be gained from words like 'king' or 'judge' or 'shepherd'; but, if taken too seriously, they lead to a localization of God which is disastrous.

The only image of God which I find useful is the air 'in which we live and move and have our being'. Fortunately it is difficult to represent pictorially.

GOD IN HUMAN TERMS

'People today are put off by the crude anthropomorphism with which the Church continues to speak of God.'

WHY DO you regard anthropomorphism as crude? It means, in a religious context, portraying or describing God in terms of human qualities or characteristics.

Man is, at his best, the highest, noblest, most intricate and most interesting phenomenon on this earth. He has the power of reasoning and of moral judgement; he is capable of creation as an artist, and, as the artist of his own life, of creating a noble character. Above all, he is capable of love.

If we present God in terms of man-at-his-best we are trying to explain him in terms of something with which we are all intimately familiar, and which is the highest known entity at our disposal. I cannot see that there is anything crude about that.

And what are the alternatives? If we de-personalize our metaphors and try to explain God in terms of something like energy, we are obliged to draw our imagery from electricity, or internal combustion, or nuclear fission. I would have thought that these, although they may afford certain insights, really are crude.

But perhaps you mean that we ought not to take our anthropomorphism in a crude way? I suppose that there may be people who do believe that God really has a *right hand* or *merciful ears* and things like that because they hear these words in the lessons and the liturgy. I can only say that I have never to my knowledge met such a person.

I think that there may be even an element of unconscious intellectual snobbery behind the desire to abandon 'crude anthropomorphism'. We must remember that God has to be all things to all men. Jesus taught us through his parables that a farm-hand sowing his corn or a housewife sweeping a room can gain, through those simple activities, an insight into the Kingdom of Heaven. Faith must never be allowed to become some rarefied intellectual exercise, or it will be out of reach to the greater part of mankind.

This is the supreme value of that great act of anthropomorphism which we celebrate at Christmas. The fact that God took on a human body and a human mind is in itself an endorsement of the age-long practice of describing God in human terms.

It is highly relevant, also, to the great commandment – to love God. Tell me to love the underlying principle behind reality, and I am at a loss to know how to set about it. Tell me to love the Infant at Bethlehem or the Man in Galilee or at Golgotha, and I can do something about it.

N.B. The same point which I made in the previous article about the danger of localizing God needs to be remembered.

CHANCE AND DIVINE CONTROL

'Cardinal Hume, in a TV interview, said that the death of the late Pope John Paul I was according to the will of God. If God is responsible for the termination of a human life at an appointed time, can we justify any medical activity that seeks to postpone death?'

IF THE Cardinal is saying that God sometimes intervenes in the course of nature and arranges for this or that person to die at a particular time, I find this possible to accept in principle, though difficult if not impossible to define in practice. It is a little presumptuous to claim to know the inmost thoughts of God.

If, however, the Cardinal is saying that everybody's death takes place at a moment decided by God, then we are on very different ground. I would find it difficult to believe in God, and in particular in the justice and goodness of God, if I had to accept this as true.

We all know the tale: infants not allowed even to become children; young lives cut off in their prime; good, useful lives suddenly put to an end; old, useless lives agonizingly prolonged. It is impossible for me to see any rhyme or reason, let alone justice, in it.

It may be urged against me that God, in his wisdom, knows far better than I do and that, if I knew the full facts, then I would recognize the justice which in my ignorance I fail to see. There is obviously some solid sense in this; we must certainly aim off considerably for human ignorance.

But there is grave danger in taking this argument to the point at which you have to say: 'God's justice is so superior to human justice that what *seems* unjust to us *is* just to him.' If my black may be God's white, what grounds have I for avoiding it? If my white may be God's black, what possible incentive have I for pursuing the idea of the good in this life? Have I, indeed, any grounds for supposing that the word 'good' has any recognizable meaning?

Human justice, with all its imperfections, must be identifiably *of the same nature* as God's justice. We may lag far behind but we must know that we are on the same road.

This leaves us with the further alternative - that chance is part of God's scheme for his creation. I think that chance is all part of human freedom, which is a necessity if

morals are to have any meaning and love any value. A
world in which every event was dictated by God would
doubtless be devoid of evil. But human beings would be
reduced to the status of puppets, and their actions thereby
emptied of moral value.

MADE IN THE IMAGE OF GOD

*'What does it mean to say that man is made in the image of
God?'*

THIS IS one of the many sayings in the Bible which are not
explained. Another is the requirement to be like little
children. They invite the immediate question: 'in what way?'
The very fact that no explanation is given forces us to
make use of our imaginations. Again and again these
sayings will 'come to life' as some new experience opens our
eyes to some new facet of their meaning.

One of the most obvious interpretations to put on the
phrase *image of God* is to take from its context in Genesis
the idea of God as essentially the Creator. If we are made
in his image, we too can create.

There is, however, one important difference. God's act
of creation was the only truly original act of creation. He
created from nothing. 'We are never the real creators,'
wrote Yves Congar in his *Priest and Layman*; 'all we can do
is transform and set in motion the gifts which God has made
to us,' He goes on to point out that, because we are not
truly creators, we are never absolute owners.

That consideration is very important, especially when we
are applying our thinking to 'test-tube babies' and that
sort of issue. But I suppose it is the artist who gets
nearest to true creation. The theme is well worked out for
the art of the writer in Dorothy L. Sayers' *The Mind of the
Maker*, a book which I can only commend to you. But this
creativity extends to the whole ability to create the sort of
truth which Keats identified with beauty - whether in
words, or form, or sound, or colour, or movement.

But God is not merely Creator. He is also described as
being Love. Here, I think, we are on fairly obvious
ground. When we are truly loving we are demonstrating
that we are truly made in the image of God. But many
other things - especially possessiveness, indulgence and
sentimentality - can masquerade as love; and we need the

example as well as the words of Christ to remind us that the highest expression of love is in sacrifice. At the very least there is a sterner side to love which is a little out of fashion today. This reminds us that love often goes with 'chastening', which at least means discipline, even if it does not mean 'chastising'.

But there are other facets of the idea of man made in the image of God which I hope will occur to you as you think about it.

GROUND OF BEING

'I believe in God, but I find it difficult to believe in a personal God.'

AND *I* find it impossible to believe in anything less! I don't quite know what it is that people find so attractive about obscure phrases - 'unmoved mover', 'elan vital', 'principle of reality' - unless it is that they *want* the nature of this fundamental being to remain obscure. These are all evasive phrases.

It is possible also that there is something about a personal God which sticks in your throat. Does it seem to make God too small, too comprehensible? Does it conjure up in your mind the idea that God is just another *bloke*, albeit writ large?

If so, then we must consider what it is we mean by calling him 'personal'. It is basically a question of whether the word 'God' (or any of the substitutes for it) is to remain a sort of intellectual cypher - something which you assume for purposes of argument and can ignore if you do not join in the argument - or whether God is capable of being the object of some sort of relationship. The former keeps him safely within the sphere of speculation: the latter can transform one's life.

The moment we try to put any content to the word 'God', we embark upon theology. Is he the Creator? Because, if so, there are strong reasons for attributing to him the possession of something which we must call mind. Certainly, if creation has any purpose behind it, it must proceed from mind. What is his relationship to this creation? It could be that of puppet-master to puppet show. If we *could* pray to such a master, it would have to be on the lines of the prayer in *The Lady's not for Burning*:

'Almighty God, more precise than any clockmaker: grant us all a steady pendulum.'

But, if God has introduced freedom into his creation, then the personal quality of his nature becomes enhanced. Because freedom introduces the possibility of sin – of things going wrong with creation. How does an *élan vital* deal with sin? If he deals with it either by punishment or forgiveness, or by incarnation and atonement, we are well launched into the vocabulary of personality. But it is only a vocabulary. We can apply the metaphors of king or judge or, better still, of father. This brings with it the highly personal attribute of love.

But the important thing is that these are metaphors and not definitions. I forget who said *un Dieu defini est un Dieu fini* – but he was right. A God who can be defined has ceased to be God.

IMAGES OF FATHERHOOD

'Since "paternalism" is a dirty word today, is it helpful to think of God any longer as "Father"?'

LET US TAKE a similar example first. *Nepotism* has been a dirty word for a long time. I believe that the term derives from the practice of certain medieval Popes whose nephews – or whose illegitimate sons known euphemistically as nephews – were heaped with unmerited honours.

But this pejorative sense of the word *nepotism* in no way impugnes the ordinary uncle/nephew relationship. In my own childhood, when the word *father* still had disciplinary connotations which it has largely lost today, uncles were popular figures with children; and indeed, for some, the word *avuncular* has strong overtones of benevolence.

The fact, therefore, that *paternalism* is a dirty word does not disturb me. It could leave the true image of fatherhood untarnished. What does matter, when we are thinking of the fatherhood of God, is that we should have some vision vouchsafed us of an ideal fatherhood at human level. Our subconscious images of 'Father' may vary greatly.

In Pont's immortal series of cartoons, *Popular Misconceptions*, there was one entitled 'Life when Father was a Boy'. It shows Paterfamilias and his son in a very Oxbridge-looking study adorned with Landseer prints and public-school trophies. The son is standing on a carefully selected pile of books which elevate him sufficiently, when bent over with his head under the table, to offer a convenient target to father's birch, which one can see – thanks to the artist's matchless mastery of expression – is being applied more in sorrow than in anger.

The opposite extreme I could illustrate from an occasion in my pastoral experience when I called on a family in a housing estate. Dad opened the door with the familiar 'was there something?' expression. On this occasion there *was* something: their son was in trouble with the police. 'I've called about John,' I said. 'Oh,' answered Dad with evident relief: 'you want to see his Mum.' And therewith he abdicated. I lacked the courage to point out to him that a negative non-entity of a father combined with a possessive and dominating mother is the best recipe for producing a homosexual yet discovered.

Another form of abdication consists in the disclaimer against any right to 'mould' the character of one's children – a task which this century prefers to entrust to the clay itself and not to the potter. But how we do love to select inapt metaphors!

Fathers are not like potters; they should be like gardeners. A gardener does not *mould* a chrysanthemum; but he does put a lot of loving care into the business of providing the best possible conditions in which that delicate plant can grow. I would like to see the Church leading a real revival of the role of father. Seen at its best, the father/child relationship is one of the most attractive I know.

THE FATHERHOOD OF GOD

'I hear that the Church in America is trying to get rid of all masculine vocabulary in talking of God. Surely he is our Father?'

I DO not see how there can be any *objective* truth in any language which attributes masculinity to God. Such language could only be meaningful ultimately in the physical terms of genitals and hormones.

To call God 'Father' is not to claim for him any of the physical prerequisites for procreation. It is to use a metaphor or a simile in which an insight may be obtained into the nature of God from the comparison with the relationship of father and child. Jesus Christ presumably used the word 'father' deliberately, and meant thereby something which could not have been equally well expressed by the word 'mother'. You might wish to add: 'in an age that put a very different meaning to the word "mother" because of its ignorance of genetics.'

However, if Jesus used a metaphor from masculinity, it cannot be wrong to follow suit. But we must not press the metaphor too far.

That men and women are equally in the image of God – who can therefore be neither male nor female exclusively – seems to be made clear by Genesis 5:2 (it is amazing how few people read as far as this!): 'In the likeness of God made he him; male and female created he *them*, and called *their* name Adam.' 'Adam' in Hebrew means 'mankind'.

The English language is weak here in only having one word – 'man' – for what is expressed by two different words in Greek: aner = 'male', and anthropos = 'the human race'. When we say 'man', therefore, in English, we do not necessarily specify masculinity.

The problem is acuter also for the English than for the French. It was possible to refer to the King of France as *elle* if, in the previous sentence, he had been described as *sa Majesté*. 'Majesty' happens to be a feminine noun, and the French find no difficulty in applying it to a masculine person.

THE WHEREABOUTS OF GOD

'Christians still seem to cling to the idea that God is "out there".'

YOU SEEM to take it for granted that they are wrong. There is in fact nothing wrong or misleading with the idea that God is 'out there', provided that it is not coupled with the thought, however dimly present to the mind, that God is a finite being who can be located in space and therefore must be either here or there.

A number of people seem to cut God down to human size and human limitations as a preliminary to withdrawing their belief from him. There is no reason for making the very common step from regarding God as out there to regarding God as being away from it all. As ever, a great deal depends upon the metaphors and images which we use to formulate the concept.

I often used to illustrate the Trinity in my confirmation classes by means of the sun. We can think of it as the actual *thing*: then there is the light by means of which it is made visible to us; and finally there is the life-giving and life-sustaining power actively at work in the vegetable and animal kingdoms.

The sun is, fortunately, both out there and up there. This does not prevent its having an all-important influence on what happens down here, and on the atmosphere in which we live and move and have our being. A student of the sun might well have to concentrate in two directions - the world around him in which the sun is at work, and the flaming ball *out there* from which the influence comes.

It seems to me that, if God were simply and only to be found 'in the human situation' - and in one's own inner self and in one's fellow-creatures - there would be little point in the Incarnation and the Trinity.

Of the Incarnation it was said that 'God *sent* his only Son.' The whole idea of sending suggests a degree of remoteness: you do not need to send if you are already fully present. And Jesus himself, in the words of St John, talked of *leaving* his disciples and *going to the father.* This also suggests the idea of remoteness in the Father. But he promised to *send* another Comforter, the Holy Spirit. All this language is really meaningless if we abolish the whole idea of God being 'out there'.

The language of transcendence has, I need hardly add, to be balanced by the language of immanence. In many ways God is within us and among us; and a doctrine, or a liturgy, which leans excessively to one or the other view must be regarded as lop-sided.

THE REALITY OF GOD

'I often come to Church but I never seem to feel the reality of God.'

I ONCE knew a parishioner who always sat right at the back of the Church and then complained that he could not hear me. I suggested to him, as tactfully as possible, that it might be a good idea to move up a little nearer to the source of sound.

I just wonder if your trouble may not be that you are standing too far away from God to be aware of him. Would it be a good idea to try and move a little closer in?

It might be appropriate to your predicament to consider the important saying in John 7:17, 'If any man purposes to do his will, he will know of the teaching whether it is of God.' Faith is not the affair of the intellect: it is the affair of the will. I would often advise a person to whom God seems unreal to start by *obeying* God. *Try* to love your neighbour; *try* to love your 'enemy'; *try* to forgive those who 'trespass' against you; *try* not to return evil for evil.

You will notice that I have taken you right out of Church, where you have apparently been seeking God, and into the world of human relationships. God is to be found in both, and it is dangerous to look for him exclusively in either. But if you are not getting through to him on one line, switch to the other.

To change my metaphor – I always see these as the two feet by which a Christian advances. If your 'church' foot has got stuck, put your 'world' foot forward; if your 'world' foot is stuck, put your 'church' foot forward. But whatever you do, please do not imagine that you are going to advance by hopping on one foot.

Once it gets started there is upward movement possible in the form of a spiral. It is the pure in heart who see God, but it is the vision of God which purifies the heart. Somehow you have to cut in on this cycle and get caught up in it.

I have to add that of course the expression 'see God' is not to be understood in a literal or physical manner. No man has ever seen God. It is to be understood here more as when you say that you 'see' the solution to a problem. People's awareness of God takes many different forms, and I have no room to expand on this here. But you might ask yourself: 'What am I really expecting this "feeling the reality of God" to be?'

STILL THE SAME GOD

'It seems to me that the Old Testament gives a very different idea of God from the New. Is God supposed to have changed?'

I DO NOT see any need to infer that God has changed at any stage in history. It is far more likely that it was the people's attitude towards him that changed.

We are given, on the highest authority, the simile of a father to illumine our understanding of God. Let us see what this simile will yield in this case.

A very small child might regard a father as a delightful person to play with; later he might learn to treat him as a disciplinary force to be reckoned with. Later still he could grow into a relationship of real and mutual friendship.

And of course the father will be mediating himself to the child in a different way at each successive age. It is a lesson that some parents never learn, but that is beside the point. At a certain age a child needs a firm discipline imposed from without as a framework within which to grow. At a later stage he needs to he helped to grow into freedom and responsibility. So the father will provide law at one stage and withdraw it progressively at another. It is not the father who is changing, but the needs of the child.

This is just what St Paul says of God the Father in Galatians. The law, he says, was a tutor to bring man to Christ - but, when man is grown up enough, the tutor's work will have come to an end. I don't think that you will make any sense of the Old Testament and its relationship with the New except on these lines.

In the case to which you refer in your letter - our Lord's handling of the Ten Commandments - I think that the matter is rather more complex. Jesus specifically stated that he came to *fulfil* the law and not to abolish it.

The law dealt - as law must always deal - with *actions*: thou shalt not commit murder; thou shalt not commit adultery. Jesus was laying down the principles which lie behind the law; he was dealing with morality and not with law.

It may be immoral to commit adultery with someone in your heart; God help us all if it ever became illegal. But, in transferring his hearers' attention from the law to the moral principles behind it, our Lord was certainly treating them as more mature people.

DIVINE AUTHORITY

'You wrote: "Absolute authority only too often becomes tyranny". Does not God possess absolute authority?'

I WAS talking, of course, of authority as exercised by

human beings, not of the authority of God.

It is interesting to note the difference in the meaning of the word 'authority' as used in the New Testament. The primary meaning of the Greek word *exousia* is 'power of choice' or 'liberty of action'. This is illustrated in Acts 5:4 when Ananias withheld some of his money from the apostles – 'was it not still *at your own disposal*?' (NEB). Or again in I Corinthians 8:9 – 'be careful that this *liberty* of yours does not become a pitfall for the weak.'

In Mark 1:22 Jesus is described as 'teaching as one having authority and not as the Scribes.' The Scribes, however, were the authorized teachers of the law; so here we have an opposition between two kinds of authority, the authority which derives from the ring of truth in a person's inner being and the authority which consists in laying down the law.

Lastly, there is the famous passage in Mark 10:43 about the rulers of the Gentiles 'making the weight of their authority felt.' Our Lord is unequivocal about that: it is forbidden to Christians.

If we turn to the Latin we get closer to your question. The word from which we get 'author' and 'authority' is *auctor*. Its primary meaning is 'one who makes a thing grow.'

Now this is precisely the sort of authority which I would attribute to God. My favourite image of the Christian leader is that of the gardener. It is based on I Corinthians 3:6 – 'I have planted; Apollos watered; but God gave the growth.' That seems to me to pinpoint the difference between human and divine authority. The one thing which a gardener does not and cannot do is to make a plant grow; he can only provide conditions favourable for growth.

There is a helpful passage on authority in a little booklet on the agreed statement of the Anglican-Roman Catholic International Commission (ARCIC) by E.J. Yarnold and Henry Chadwick. 'Most characteristically it stands for an invitation and a summons to men to exercise their freedom in ways indicated by the bearer of authority. Even God, from whom all authority is derived, seeks from men free obedience, not forced servitude. When, on the contrary, authority relies too heavily on compulsion, it lapses into what is called authoritarianism.'

REVERENCE - AND RESPECT FOR GOD

*'One doesn't seem to notice so much reverence in church
these days. Has all respect for God been abolished?'*

I HOPE not - but I wonder what it is that you are looking
for as the outward signs of reverence. Many people have a
most inadequate idea of what reverence is.

I remember one old woman, who was bedridden, refusing
to have Holy Communion celebrated in her bedroom because
it would be 'shockingly irreverent'. In her view reverence
was wholly a question of externals. The teaching of Jesus
Christ is that we must give total priority to the internal
state of heart and mind. If this is right, we can leave the
external expression to take care of itself.

One of the Greek words translated *reverence* in the New
Testament is *eulabeia*. Literally it means 'handling well'. If
you have ever seen a connoisseur of art handling one of his
treasures you will understand the primary meaning of the
word. By the loving care with which he treats the object he
proclaims its value in his eyes - its worth-ship, which is
the same as worship. Worship and reverence are not really
separable in thought.

If you put the word *reverence* into German you get
Ehrfurcht - a typical German compound meaning 'honour-
fear'. It is very different from being frightened. To be
frightened of God is the re-action of an ignorant savage.
To experience honour-fear is to recognize the majesty of
the Almighty God.

I think that one of the troubles today may be that we
have lost almost all sense of honour-fear for other people.
If we do not experience the feeling in our human
relationships, we may have nothing to translate into terms
of our relations with God. 'He that loveth not his brother
whom he hath seen, how can he love God whom he hath not
seen?'

This loss of reverence for other people may be connected
with the general collapse of authority in our time. But
there is no need to connect honour-fear with authority. St
Francis leaping from his horse to kiss a leper, or Bishop
Myriel in *Les Misérables* addressing the escaped convict as
'Sir' - these are just as much examples of reverence: what
Albert Schweitzer called 'reverence for life'. It is due to a
person by virtue of the fact that he was created by God in
his image, by virtue of the fact that Christ died for him.

If our congregations were to attain such mutual regard for one another, and the fellowship of the Holy Spirit could become a reality in our acts of worship, I think that a more vivid sense of the worth-ship of God might be realized in our services - and a vivid sense of God is the inner reality of reverence.

Doctrine

PURPOSE OF LIFE

'Does Religion get any support from Philosophy?'

THIS IS rather a large subject to ask anyone to condense
into four hundred words. 'Philosophy' covers a great range
of often discordant opinions. 'Religion' is perhaps a little
easier to define. I offer a definition from Stafford Clark: 'A
quest of the purpose of life and for the individual's place
in that purpose.'

One might go a stage further and say it was a quest for
the meaning of life. The basic idea is that you cannot
understand anything until you have discovered its purpose.
Just imagine how baffled you would be by your first

confrontation with a piano if you were stone deaf and
unaware of the existence of music. You would be unable to
answer the question: 'What is all this elaborate mechanism
for?' Until you understand the purpose you cannot
understand the thing.

The same argument can be applied to life, which includes
your life. If this is a chance by-product of an impersonal,
self-creating process, it is useless to seek its purpose, for
purpose presupposes mind. You could hardly imagine a
piano existing or coming into existence without having first
been conceived in the mind of a musician.

The argument, then, is that, if life has a purpose, it
must be the product of a mind; and the attempt to
discover, and to get into communication with, this mind is
the basic urge of religion. By this view faith is, in the
first place, a refusal to accept that life is meaningless
although logically there is no reason why it should not be
so.

A number of other important ideas follow from this first
concept of purpose. One is in the realm of revelation. If
God made life and has a purpose for the universe and for
you, then it would be expected that he would make his
purpose known. A God of purpose is almost bound to be a
God of revelation. The detached and unapproachable God of
the Theist is not logically probable.

Secondly, the idea of purpose gives us a clue to the
vocabulary of ethics. The word 'good' is perfectly easily
understood in a non-ethical context. There is hardly room
for argument as to what the word means in the phrase 'a
good rifle'; there is endless argument as to what it means
in the phrase 'a good man'. But a good rifle is one which
fulfils the purpose for which a rifle is designed. So, in the
same sense, a good man would be one who fulfilled the
purpose for which God had created him; and we would
expect this purpose to be part of the revelation of God.

The concept of purpose can be taken further into the
realm of ethics when we are trying to appraise (which is a
form of understanding) not a man but an action. Once again
we have to take into account the purpose - or, as we would
say in this case, the motive - for doing it. An action can
only be fully good when the motive for doing it is good
also.

N.B. For the importance of purpose, see William Temple
Nature, Man and God, *at the end of lecture VIII.*

FAITH & REASON

'Surely faith is all emotion and no reason?'

I WOULD have said that there were two sides to an act of faith. One is the sort of total response to a person which we experience when we fall in love: it is quite inadequate to call it 'emotional', although of course the emotions are fully involved. The other is a rational understanding of the situation which distinguishes true belief from belief in fairies or Father Christmas.

By a rational understanding of, for instance, the Incarnation – the act whereby 'he came down to earth from Heaven' – I mean the ability to make sense of it, and I would do it thus: we are all familiar these days with the *problem of communication*. Put at its simplest, people of one sort find it difficult to get across to people of another sort; they don't 'speak the same language'.

Whatever you may think of the priests who became industrial workers, the theory on which they were acting was intelligent and intelligible. The priest wants to get across to the worker – so what does he do? He *becomes* one; he learns to speak their language, and he earns the right to be listened to. 'Becoming one' is the essence of the Incarnation, and it involves sharing to the full in the sufferings of the group with which you thus identify yourself.

I remember when I was living in France, not long after the war, hearing the phrase, 'you don't understand; you didn't suffer.' There is a confraternity of suffering, and the indispensable qualification for entrance is to have suffered yourself. In this way we can begin to see how inevitably the Incarnation led to the Passion. Jesus Christ could not have identified himself with us fully if he had not shared in the worst of our sufferings.

You might almost say that, in creating Man with free will and the consequent ability to sin, God created his own problem of communication, which he of course foresaw and which, after careful preparation, he remedied by the Incarnation. But, if the Incarnation has an inherent probability about it which makes it easier to accept, this is not, of course, any proof that Jesus Christ was the agent of it.

It is at this point that logic and reason must yield to what I have called 'total response' in order to complete the act of faith. This is the most difficult thing of all to explain to the unbeliever. It is like trying to explain love to someone who has never experienced it.

It would be only too easy for such a person to note the similarities between love and lust and to remain blind to the differences. He would easily assume that you were just out for what you could get. Only those who have had the real experience from inside can know how far from the truth this is.

FOR EVER & EVER?

'Isn't the idea of eternal life just wishful thinking?'

THE IMPORTANT WORD in your question is 'just'. It is very easy to insert a little word like that without due thought for its significance. It may be that the idea of eternal life *is* wishful thinking, in which case let us give close scrutiny to wishful thought.

I often hear quoted in this context a saying which I believe originates in Auguste Comte – 'nor does being hungry prove that we are going to have bread'. At face value this is merely a truism which is hardly worth the stating, but those who believe that it discredits the idea of eternal life are guilty of an error in logic.

Of course the feeling of hunger does not prove that anyone is going to *have* bread, any more than the hunger for eternal life proves that any particular individual is going to *receive* that either. But this is not the point at issue. The point at issue is whether it *exists*.

We do not have to argue the existence of food, so the parallel is a stupid one, but I would certainly regard it as strange, if human beings were so constituted as *not* to require food and lived in a world where there was no such thing as food, to find them experiencing hunger. If any argument *were* needed, the fact of hunger is argument *for*, not against, the existence of food.

The fact that the greater part of mankind throughout the ages has been reluctant to accept mortality and has experienced a 'hunger' for eternal life is, if anything, a *prima facie* ground for supposing that the means of satisfying this hunger exist. It is, of course, no proof. But it would be absurd to argue that, simply because we do desire it, it therefore does not exist.

But what do we *mean* when we say a 'desire for eternity'? I am often surprised at the number of people who do not want immortality because they persist in seeing it as an indefinite extension of *this* life. The pearly gates open – and there is Mum having one of her off days. For most people three score and ten years of the imperfections of this world ought to be quite enough. Why *should* man wish for more?

I can only find an answer in the concept that the good, the beautiful and the true are intrinsically worthy of eternity. The bad, the ugly and the false are by definition in need of changing and are by nature temporary. I believe that the mainspring of most great art is the desire to eternalize something which is transient, because we cannot accept that something which is beautiful should be allowed to *be* transient.

What some people dismiss as 'wishful thinking' turns out to be profound moral reasoning.

THE FIRE THAT PURIFIES

'Is not the idea of Hell Fire morally repulsive?'

SOME OF THE EMBROIDERY upon the theme, both in medieval art and in nineteenth-century preaching, is certainly repulsive. Brother Amos's sermon to the Quivering Brethren in *Cold Comfort Farm* is hardly a burlesque. But, if we confine ourselves to the New Testament, we narrow the field considerably.

It is chiefly a question of what interpretation we give to the word 'fire'. The word can be used in a rich variety of metaphors, and one of the most suggestive comes from Malachi 3:2, 'He is like a refiner's fire ... He shall purify.'

The word 'purify' is properly used of the process whereby the dross is burned out of gold ore, leaving only the *pure* gold. I can see nothing morally offensive about the removal of all in a human being that is unworthy to stand before God eternally. If we are going to take all our selfish little ways with us into the next world, heaven will be no better than earth.

The next question is to ask how this process of purification is to be accomplished? Is the selfish side of us *literally* burned out of us? Is the process one of cauterization? There is at least one text, the parable of the

Sheep and the Goats, which links the idea of fire with that of punishment.

We seem rather to have lost belief in punishment these days, but this may be at root a loss of confidence in our own ability to judge. Phrases such as 'cruel only to be kind' or 'this is going to hurt me more than you' are apt to be dismissed as hypocrisy. But I think that the present reaction against the over-severity of the past generation has already gone too far and that the Church must stand for the fact that it is possible and necessary for Love to punish. Undoubtedly this is the Biblical view. But in any case you cannot argue that what is true of imperfect humanity is necessarily true of God. Even if *we* cannot punish there is no reason why *He* cannot.

But there remains a further interpretation of 'fire' which I find intriguing. It comes from the Proverbs and is quoted by St Paul to the Romans. 'If your enemy hunger, feed him ... and you will heap coals of fire upon his head.' Even the most hardened literalist could scarcely be expected to fetch a shovel and to carry out this advice *au pied de la lettre*. The meaning is suggested from one's own experience. If one's 'enemy' is kind to one, one's reaction is shame – *burning* shame. And, of course, a sense of shame is one of the greatest purifying forces we know.

It may be that, when we are confronted with the picture of ourselves in the searing light of God's truth, all that is unworthy of Him will shrivel up by the burning shame of that confrontation. The important thing to remember is that the process can and should begin in this life.

DOCTRINE, DOUBT AND THE GOSPEL

'With so much hesitation and doubt about doctrine in the Church we cannot preach any gospel. Is it surprising we make so few converts?'

THERE DOES seem to be a real difficulty here. If you look at your own beliefs from the point of view of your own integrity, you are almost certain to have hesitations and doubts in some areas unless you refuse to allow them to enter your mind, which is both dangerous and stupid. Doubt must be faced honestly, and your personal faith will emerge the stronger for having been exercised in this way.

Thomas Merton has said: 'Faith is a principle of

questioning and struggle before it becomes a principle of certitude and peace ... one's faith itself must be tested and purified. Christianity is not merely a set of foregone conclusions.'

I think you are saying that Christians ought to present a set of foregone conclusions to the world in order to convert it. I know that many people would like to hear the Church giving positive answers where it seems only to be asking questions itself. Many people *would* like to be relieved of the responsibility for thought, of 'questioning and struggle'. It has to be asked, however, whether it would be healthy for their faith to give them these certitudes.

I think it must depend upon which truths you have in mind. At the heart of any faith that is worth the name, there must be *some* absolute conviction.

The gospel – the Good News – is a fairly brief and simple portion of the whole body of Christian teaching. It asserts the action of God, that 'while we were yet sinners Christ died for the ungodly'; it knocks away the idea that we get our deserts: 'he hath not dealt with us after our sins, nor rewarded us according to our wickednesses.' It asserts that this is achieved for us by Christ's sacrifice on the Cross; that we are offered a union with Christ so close that we can be said to die with him and rise to new life.

All this is the gospel. Anyone who has experienced any of its impact will have no doubts in his inmost heart as to the reality of the power and therefore the truth of the doctrine that recognizes and asserts that power.

When you mention 'preaching' the gospel, it is important to stress that no amount of verbal affirmation of the things I have listed above is likely to have any converting power, however uncompromisingly stated, unless it has first converted the speaker. We preach with our lives far more than with our words.

FORMULAS WITHOUT MEANING?

'I feel that the old formulas of the Christmas narratives have lost their meaning. It is difficult to know how to present Christmas except in terms of outworn orthodoxy.'

WE MUST NOT put the cart before the horse. Religious experience comes first; theologising about that experience

comes second. If one generation's theologising has become
'outworn' or unsatisfactory to a new generation, the work
may have to be re-done. But the basic experience without
which no theologising could have been provoked remains the
same. It is the experience of God.

This is put quite clearly by the late Professor Lampe.
'The first Christians did not enquire, as the Greek
philosophical theologians were later to ask, what was the
relation of the essential being of Jesus Christ to that of
God the Father. They were concerned for what he did.'

Their experience of Jesus was an experience of new life;
of release from the inhibiting forces of the world, release
from the 'slavery' of sin, release from the shackles of
legalism. Later reflection led them to see in the quite
unique authority claimed by Christ, both in the 'signs'
which he performed and in his attitude towards the law and
to the forgiveness of sins, a truly divine nature.

One of the earliest classical expressions of this is the
opening chapter of St John's Gospel, which is rightly used
as the Christmas gospel: 'The Word was made flesh and
dwelt among us.'

The spiritual and psychological importance of this was
seen by the author of the Epistle to the Hebrews (how I
wish that *that* was the epistle for Christmas!): 'We have not
a High Priest who cannot be touched with the feeling of our
infirmities, but was in all points tempted like as we are,
yet without sin.' Those who have not felt the strength and
comfort of this acknowledgement are still 'afar off'.

I think, therefore, that Christmas services should seek
not so much to present the formulas of orthodoxy as to try
to evoke the experience which underlies them. If the Word
was made *flesh* - if God is to be found *in* man and has
made his final revelation of himself *through* man - then
there could be no more powerful symbol than that most
fundamental of all human scenes, a mother with her baby.

It should be a matter of great inspiration that, at the
very heart of our religion, we should have so intensely
human a scene.

*N.B. This was written before the 'Bishop of Durham
controversy' which has most recently provoked the
report by the House of Bishops* The Nature of Christian
Belief.

THE WORD BECAME FLESH

*'How can those who do not believe in the Virgin Birth
celebrate Christmas?'*

'AND THE WORD became flesh and dwelt among us,' said St
John. It *became* flesh. The Greek word translated 'became'
can also mean 'was born'.

William Temple makes the point that the Word did not
just indwell or occupy a human form; it was fully identified
with human nature. That, I think, is our common ground
and the basis of what we all can celebrate at Christmas. I
can see no ground in St John either for accepting the
Nativity stories as historical or not. He does not raise the
question *how* the Word became flesh.

I would not myself attempt to define the relationship
between the two statements that Jesus is 'perfect God and
perfect man'. I forget who said *'un Dieu defini est un Dieu
fini'* (which I would render loosely 'a God who can be
defined has ceased to be God'), but I wholly agree with it.

I content myself with two ideas which are, to me,
indispensable. One is that Jesus is a proper object of
worship and therefore *is* God. The other is that 'we have
not a High Priest who cannot be touched with the feeling of
our infirmities, but was in all points tempted like as we
are.' Jesus *was* man. To ask how these two statements
relate to each other seems to me to come very near to
trying to define God.

I would like to quote from *Reasonable Belief*, by A. and
R. Hanson (1981). 'In Luke the account is cast in poetic
rather than in historical language.' They continue: 'the
Virgin Birth story, it is held, explains how he is both man
and God: he had Mary for a mother and God for a father.'
But from this 'we must conclude that he was half man and
half God. Modern biology has shown that the embryo is the
product of both the male and the female. Ancient
embryology mistakenly held that the female merely provided
the receptacle: it was the male who created the new being'.

In this case it is difficult to see how those who held this
mistaken view could have believed Jesus to be even half
man. It can therefore hardly have been for this reason that
the stories gained acceptance.

Those who disbelieve the historicity of the Virgin Birth
do so by rejecting a 'literal' interpretation of the texts. It
is possible to accuse them of something akin to literalism in

holding that the normal rules of embryology must be applied in a case which must be regarded as a unique act of God. God is not tied by his embryology.

However, the Hansons conclude in the possibility of accepting the Virgin birth stories, but suggest that they should not be 'treated as a foundation-stone of Christian doctrine'. The absence of these stories from Mark and John and Paul require us, I think, to agree with this.

WHY DID JESUS HAVE TO DIE?

'"He died that we might be forgiven". But why did he have to die? Why cannot we just be forgiven?'

IMAGINE a court of law. The jury returns the verdict of 'guilty'. The judge gives the sentence: 'You are forgiven.' Do you feel that something is lacking here? That, at least on some occasions, such forgiving would be immoral?

If no punishment is ever imposed, nothing is done to vindicate the wrong which has been done. The word 'vindicate' comes from two Latin words, one meaning 'to say' and the other meaning 'force'. To vindicate is to state forcefully. A punishment states forcefully that something intolerable has been done.

But it is an unfortunate fact that, the worse a person is, the less punishment is likely to be effective. Every schoolmaster knows that the nice boys are easy to punish because they understand the justice of it - but that the really bad ones do not understand the justice, and resent it, and make it into fuel for deeper opposition to authority.

I think that this arises from the fact that some of the most anti-social customers are not wholly to blame for the fact that they are anti-social. A rotten environment is not conducive to a moral outlook. One feels that some people never had a chance, and that to punish them for something for which society itself is really responsible would be unjust and counter-productive. But, if they are *not* punished, what will 'say forcefully' that their anti-social behaviour is intolerable?

The Statue of Justice holds a pair of scales. This suggests that a crime upsets the balance of society. To redress the balance, something needs to be paid - re-tributed - to the other side of the scales.

In suffering upon the cross, Christ showed how much

sin matters to God – he *said it with force*; he vindicated it.
He put his own suffering on to the other half of the scales
and redressed the balance.

It was at the very moment that the nails were being
driven in that he spoke the words: 'Father, forgive them,
they know not what they do.' No one who has received his
forgiveness uttered by those lips at that moment can claim
that the forgiveness of God is immoral.

The Cross makes moral the forgiveness of God. 'He died
that we might be forgiven.' You must excuse the brevity of
my argument: it usually takes me three hours to try and
explain this one.

A UNIQUE EVENT

'What do you think happened at the Resurrection?'

I WAS greatly helped towards an understanding of this
matter by a book called *Real Resurrection*, by David van
Daalen, a member of the Dutch Reformed Church who
became a Presbyterian minister in England. He writes very
clear English, but what he says is profound. I will give a
few quotations.

'Human searching, if it is really honest, sincere and
critical, can only end in profound agnosticism. There is no
way from us to God.'

'Either Christ was raised from the dead, or he was not.
But no argument, no reasoning, no research, no experiment
will bring the truth to light. Either he is beyond human
searching, or he would be a mere resuscitated corpse; and
that would be the very opposite of the Living Lord. Yet
there were those who saw him who cannot be seen, there
are those who met him who cannot be found and knew him
who cannot be known. That is what we can call faith.'

Van Daalen makes an interesting remark about faith,
saying that the word 'tells you something about the object
of faith rather than the person who has the faith. If I say
I have faith in a person ... I mean that he is the kind of
person one can rely on.'

Finally, 'the resurrection of Christ is only known to the
Christian Faith, which itself is not a human quality or
achievement, or indeed a religious phenomenon, but cannot
be accounted for other than as a gift of God.'

It is the experience of the risen Lord that is at the

heart of the Christian faith. But the connection between the risen Lord and the empty tomb is not made clear. The empty tomb does not seem to be an essential part of the scheme, for St Paul makes no use of it. Van Daalen produces strong arguments for accepting the fact of the empty tomb as true, but underlines its comparative unimportance.

You ask: 'what happened?' The answer is that we do not know. The event was unique. Our own resurrection does not require our tombs to be empty. St Paul, in I Corinthians 15, makes it clear that we will be given a spiritual body. But there is no explanation as to what this is. I think it means that we retain identity.

MEANING OF THE TRINITY

'I find it impossible to believe the doctrine of the Trinity.'

I WONDER if you may not really mean that you do not *understand* it.

There is no reason why anyone should understand any doctrine at any particular moment of their lives. It often requires a particular experience to open one's understanding - as you might say. 'Until I met Mrs X I never knew what devotion meant.' For the speaker of those words, at any time before his meeting with Mrs X, it might be natural to say that he did not believe in devotion; but to draw any inference that *therefore* what other people have said about devotion is nonsense would be both premature and presumptuous.

It is of course desirable that a Christian should grow into full personal understanding of the beliefs of the Church. To accept these beliefs in the absence of any personal endorsement would be the most hollow conformity. But the right to individual judgement must be exercised with humility. To say, in effect, 'this thing cannot be true because I myself find no support for it in the experience of life which I have had so far' is egocentric and short-sighted. The relevant experience may yet await you.

I could not have put any content to my 'belief' in the Trinity until the experience of marriage opened my mind to a glimpse (if not to an actual understanding) of the truth of another doctrine - that 'the two shall become one flesh'. This statement now makes sense to me in a way in which it never could have when I was a bachelor. If two people have experienced what it is to become one flesh, they are well on the way to accepting the possibility of three Persons being one God.

There is another experience which obviously opened the mind of Dorothy L. Sayers to the possibility that the doctrine of the Trinity represents truth and not fantasy, and that was her own experience as a creative writer. I can but quote from her play, *The Zeal of Thy House*:

'Every work of Creation is three-fold, an earthly trinity to match the heavenly. First there is the Creative Idea, passionless, timeless, beholding the whole work complete at once, the end in the beginning: and this is the image of the Father.

'Second, there is the Creative Energy begotten of that idea, working in time from the beginning to the end, with sweat and passion, being incarnate in the bonds of matter: and this is the image of the Word.

'Third there is the Creative Power, the meaning of the work and its response in the lively soul: and this is the image of the indwelling Spirit. And these three are one, each equally in itself the whole work, whereof none can exist without the other: and this is the image of the Trinity.'

The theme is spelt out more clearly and prosaically in her book, *The Mind of the Maker*.

Worship

'LOCALIZING' GOD

'If God is everywhere all the time, is it not dangerous to localize him in certain acts (worship) and certain places (churches)? I find our worshipping far too restricting.'

THAT THERE IS a real danger in this sort of focusing of the holy I would certainly not deny, but I hope that you are not suggesting that we should feel obliged to avoid dangerous ground. You must also consider the possible dangers of the opposite position.

In a successful marriage, love must be 'omnipresent'. There can be no times when a husband and wife do not love each other. But there must inevitably be times when this love is not uppermost in their consciousness. If we put all our eggs in the basket of omnipresence, there is a real danger that love will fade. It needs its focal points.

The term 'making love' deserves our attention. It certainly does not mean creating something that is otherwise non-existent. When we make love we are giving focus to something which we recognize as being there all the time. This concept of focus also guards against any identification or equation of love with the comparatively infrequent moments of love-making.

I think that this serves as a valid illustration of the problem that you pose, because an act of worship has precisely this function of focusing. It is, indeed, because of this parallel that I think it so desirable that the Prayer Book phrase, 'with my body I thee *worship*,' should be retained in the new marriage service.*

I have previously described one of the functions of worship as the putting of God for at least one hour in the week in his proper place at the centre of our whole scheme of life. Obviously there is a danger that this can be perverted into *confining* the recognition of his centrality to one hour a week. But, once you have identified the danger, you are well on the way to overcoming it.

C.S. Lewis puts the point with his customary succinctness in one of his *Letters to Malcolm*. 'It is well to have specifically holy places, and things, and days, for without these focal points and reminders, the belief that all is holy and "big with God" will soon dwindle into a mere sentiment. But if these holy places, things and days cease to remind us, if they obliterate our awareness that all ground is holy and every bush (could we but perceive it) a Burning Bush, then these hallows begin to do harm. Hence both the necessity and the perennial danger of "religion".'

I do not know who first suggested that it was 'just as easy to worship God on a golf-links,' but I suspect that research into how often he is so worshipped would reduce the significance of the statement. I also suspect that the practice – if it does exist at all – would soon die out if he were never worshipped in church.

*As I was a member of the General Synod at the time of the Prayer Book revision debates, I blame myself for not having proposed the retention of this phrase.

WHY PRAISE GOD?

*'Why is there so much about praise in our worship? Does
God really demand it?'*

WE MUST distinguish praise from flattery. The word 'praise'
comes from the same origin as the word 'price'. 'Appraisal'
means the setting of a true price upon something – in other
words appreciating its true value or worth. It is an easy
step from worth to worth-ship, and the connection between
praise and worship is established.

I wish that we had not debased the word 'criticize' so as
almost to reduce it to fault-finding. The statement, 'He is
so critical of everything,' is hardly likely to mean that he
is addicted to praise. But the job of the critic ought to be
appraisal: appreciating the true value.

Flattery, I think, is praise offered from the wrong
motive. It is therefore always objectionable; and the sort of
people who have to be flattered do not enjoy my respect.
Therefore I could not countenance a God who demanded
flattery.

I gather from my Concordance that the root meaning of
the Hebrew word which is often translated 'praise' in the
psalms is 'to stretch out one's hands.' This is often my own
gesture when confronted with beauty either in nature or in
art. The gesture might be accompanied by some exclamation
like 'Just look at that!'

I would observe here, in parentheses, that my own
experience of praise includes a desire to communicate my
delight and share it with someone else. It is almost
frustrating to have these experiences alone. I wish that
more people who come and praise God in church felt moved
to communicate their delight to others. I would even cast
doubts on the reality of their praise if they do not.

I doubt if it is really true to say that God *demands* our
praise in any other sense than that in which a great
masterpiece 'demands' our admiration. Praise is, in fact, the
natural response to excellence. Worship is the natural
response of the creature to its Creator.

Of course, if you do not actually appreciate the
excellence of God, I cannot see that you are in a position
to praise him. But an act of worship must set forth the
proper response to God.

IS WORSHIP TOO FORMAL?

'Is there not too much formality in the worship of the Church?'

WHAT DOES the word 'formality' really mean to you? Do phrases like 'a *mere* formality' come quickly to your mind? Does the word carry overtones of boredom, insincerity or even hypocrisy?

We live in an age which has largely discarded formality. The gains are probably obvious: the losses may be less apparent. There could be times when it would be a relief to have certain prescribed forms of behaviour. I believe that mourning is one of them. The Jews, and to some extent the Scots, have maintained certain conventions which could be supportive to the bereaved.

But all the word 'formality' really means is 'according to a set form'. Applied to an act of worship, it means that it is going to follow a prescribed order. If you have ever tried to lay on an act of worship that does *not* follow a prescribed order, you will recognize how difficult it is.

I once went to preach, as I thought, at a school. When I asked what form of worship the school used I was told: 'Anything you like.' A very great deal of work had to be put into it. It may have been a good act of worship, but I would not want to have to do that every time.

I can see no reason why the Holy Spirit should be more amenable to those who wish to worship extempore than to those who carefully prepare what they are going to do. I believe that the Holy Spirit responds to sincerity wherever it is found.

An act of worship that is formal is one which follows a prescribed form. It does not have to be dull or pompous or hollow, though it can easily become any of these. But it offers this advantage: that, if you know what is to come, you can prepare for it.

Formal worship depends on preparation more than we realize. It offers a framework into which you can insert your proper contribution. There is going to be a confession - you can only make this sincere if you have spent some time before-hand thinking what it is that *you* have to confess. Likewise this is true of thanksgiving and intercession.

All that I think that we need is to be alert to the dangers of formalism, for they are very real. It is possible to grind through the rigmarole of a Prayer Book service without its ever once touching your heart.

POWER OF SYMBOLS

'Is not the practice of venerating the cross a form of idolatry?'

WE DO ILL if we ignore the potential power of symbols. Take a secular example, such as a flag. I do not know who first invented a flag or when, but whoever first hit on the idea must have known a lot about the human soul.

History is full of evidence that what to a prosaic, cynical or literal mind, is merely two square yards of material can be imbued with a significance which has great power. Men have risked and even sacrificed their lives to save a flag. That little piece of cloth has the ability to put courage into a coward, to draw out unexpected depths of heroism in an apparent nonentity. It represents the honour of his country or his regiment, and all his loyalty can be evoked in its defence.

There was originally a merely practical reason for Trooping the Colour. It was done to show every man what the standard looked like to which he would have to rally. But, at a far deeper psychological level, it was a powerful force to attach his loyalty and draw out his devotion.

The last scene of the French Monarchy was centred entirely on two flags. In 1871 the Comte de Chambord was offered the crown of France as Henri V. But he could not accept the tricolor flag of the Revolution. He was as devoted to the white flag of the Bourbons as France was devoted to its symbol of liberation from tyranny. Flags are as important as that.

A person also can acquire this symbolic power – this ability to stand for a country or a cause. For this reason alone I am glad to live under a monarchy. For this reason among others I am glad to belong to an episcopal Church.

Christianity would be ill-advised to ignore the power of its central symbol, the cross. The purpose of a procession is to parade the cross before the people, just as Trooping the Colour paraded the standard before the troops; and, just as the troops saluted the flag, so should a congregation reverence the cross.

Reverencing a symbol is quite different from worshipping a creature, which is the definition of idolatry. Worship may indeed be offered to the Creator only, but reverence may and must be accorded to any recognized symbol or symbolic person that stands for the Creator's cause.

HYMNS WITH EVERYTHING

'Why do we sing so many hymns?'

AS GOOD an answer as any comes from George Wither in the early seventeenth-century: 'By song, matters of moment may not only be committed to memory but be more delightfully preserved unforgotten.'

Wither himself apparently set out to provide a hymn for every conceivable circumstance in life. Among 389 contingencies provided for, we find a hymn *for one upbraided with Deformity*, one *for encouraging Sick Persons to be willing to die*, one *for a Widow deprived of a loving Yoke-Fellow*, and, in case this were inappropriate, one *for a Widow delivered from a troublesome Yoke-Fellow*. Many of Wither's hymns were really soliloquies set to music – such as one to be sung *whilst we are Washing* – and this in an age that did not enjoy the acoustics of a modern bathroom.

But for most people a hymn is a corporate effort. It is worth considering on what other occasions a group of people, most of whom have no particular talent for music, would, without acute embarrassment, sing. I can only think of the Old School Song, the National Anthem or its political opposite, and various types of community singing.

Singing is one of the very few corporate activities which succeed. Corporate recitation of any length is not very satisfactory. I have never known the General Thanksgiving to 'come off' as a corporate expression of feeling. It would stand no comparison with a large congregation joining lustily in 'Now thank we all our God.' Most people are too inhibited to shout in church, and thanksgiving needs to be pitched higher emotionally than a muttered incantation.

Of course the corporate activity is valuable in itself, and not merely as a vehicle for our joy or gratitude. It both expresses and helps to create a sense of community and, as in the Old School Song or National Anthem, it both expresses and helps to create loyalty. As the blurb to the record 'Reflection on hymns for our times' puts it: 'a hymn should enable a worshipping community to express its own Christian response to God together.'

But I would like to go back to George Wither. For it is also in hymns that the basic doctrines of the Christian Church are 'preserved unforgotten.' Architectural historians have described the prolific statuary of the west fronts of Salisbury and Wells cathedrals as 'the poor man's Bible' - a description which, as Osbert Lancaster has pointed out, credits the medieval pauper with more than usually keen eyesight. But surely hymns are the plain man's theology - the 'folk song', in Erik Routley's words, 'of the Church Militant'.

This does not mean that every hymn is good or its singing appropriate to all occasions. As Routley says: 'If it offends a particular congregation by making it say what ... it could not possibly be wanting to say or required to say, it fails.'

LADDERS TO HEAVEN?

'Do you think that an act of worship is enhanced by the accoutrements of art, or that bare walls are more conducive to devotion?'

THE ARGUMENT is at least as old as the twelfth century. Its protagonists then were St Bernard and Abbot Suger of St Denis. Bernard was an extreme ascetic; Suger drew up a milder regime for his monks. What Bernard was saying might be summed up in the equation, 'Set your mind on things above, not on things on the earth.' What Suger was saying in effect was 'Let things on earth direct your gaze towards things above.'

At first sight they appear to be subjective positions, in which case each of us is free to choose according to taste. If you find that beautiful architecture, noble music and colourful vestments do raise your mind to things above, you will not listen to St Bernard. If you find them a distraction, that you have merely enjoyed them as such and have not got through to worshipping God, you will mistrust Suger. But there is no intrinsic reason why they may not both be right, one for one sort of person - the other for another - unless we dig deeper.

I wonder if there may not be a principle behind each of these positions which might or might not be consonant with Christianity.

Bernard talked of 'deeming as dung all that delights the

eye'. Is he confessing to Puritanism? Is he saying that the
attitude, 'Stop it: I like it,' is an expression of
Christianity? Because, if so, I would repudiate him. 'If
you, being evil, know how to give good gifts to your
children, how much more shall your Father which is in
Heaven give good things to them that ask him?'

The idea that all pleasure, as such, is contrary to
Christianity does not square with the doctrine that God is
love. It can lead to that ugly parody of religion which is
described in the memoirs of Augustus Hare, whose Victorian
parents subjected him to every cruelty in order,
presumably, to 'save' him from the snares of worldly
pleasure. I find the attitude simply revolting. If 'father' is
just a brute with a birch, what possible content can one
put into the opening words of the Lord's Prayer?

Suger's philosophy, however, is far more in keeping
with the doctrine of Creation and its New Testament
interpretation that 'everything created by God is good, and
nothing to be refused, if it be taken with thanksgiving.' I
would call this a eucharistic outlook on creation - regarding
everything in life as potential means for glorifying God.

I have only one 'rider', to add which is a warning,
chiefly to 'Catholics', that the elaborate and the ornate may
not be equated with the beautiful. There is great beauty in
simplicity.

ENJOYING ONE'S WORSHIP

*'I have often heard it said that we don't go to church to enjoy
ourselves. Ought an act of worship not to be enjoyable?'*

IT IS OF COURSE true that we do not go to church with
the *primary* motive of deriving enjoyment. A service is not
a form of entertainment. But we might well ask: if a
person has worshipped as he should and derives no
enjoyment from the process, is there not something wrong?

I was often told when I was young that I did not go to
church to enjoy myself. I was also told that I was not put
into this world to enjoy myself. But the fact is that I do
greatly enjoy being in this world, and I normally do enjoy
an act of worship. I wonder if there is not a useful parallel
from our everyday experience of life.

Holidays excepted, I don't imagine that many people set
out each day to see how much enjoyment they can get. But

very often, at the end of a working day, if you feel that
your time has been well spent, you can come home weary
but satisfied. If questioned, you might well say: 'I
thoroughly enjoyed my day.' In the same way, if you set
about the business of worship from the right motives, I
believe that you will come out of church feeling that you
have done something worthwhile, and that you are the
better for it. That feeling is at least akin to enjoyment.

This poses a problem for the writer of liturgy and for
those responsible for laying on an act of worship. It is
notoriously true that we derive more satisfaction from
accomplishing something which is difficult. Cricket is more
satisfying than tiddlywinks: bridge has more devotees than
beggar-my-neighbour: those who climb mountains get more
out of it than those who reach the summit by chair-lift.

There is therefore a strong case for not watering down
an act of worship in order to make it more easy. This may
seem a dangerous principle, but I think that more services
fail to satisfy worshippers because they are dull and seem
irrelevant than because they present too much of a
challenge. It is precisely the relevance of prayers, lessons
and sermons which will stimulate interest and active, even
if only mental, participation.

It is, in fact, necessary to ask what are the sources of
enjoyment or satisfaction proper to an act of worship.
Surely it should be primarily the sense of contact with
Almighty God, with all the purging, purifying, humbling
and reconciliation which is attendant upon this, not the
comfortable sense of repeating a well-loved routine; it
should be the sense of fellowship not only with the actual
congregation but with Christians throughout the world, not
the indulgence of our own cultural tastes - a feeling, in
short, that during that brief period at least, one has
occupied one's proper place in relation to the universe.

THE LIGHT WITHIN

*'The Church does not seem to be very attractive to new
members.'*

I OFTEN think that one of the best images of the Church is
a stained-glass window. Seen from outside it is both dull
and meaningless; its colour is drab and its forms
irrelevant. Pass inside the Church, however, and you get

the light streaming in through the window - the beauty and the meaning are at once apparent.

It is also true to say that Christianity looks more attractive from within than from without. To those who have taken the trouble to come inside and have stayed, it offers comforts and consolations, but it does not seem to have much attracting power. Like the stained-glass window, it looks drab and irrelevant to those outside.

But there are two ways in which worshippers may respond to an act of worship. The poles are represented by *passive reception and inspired action*. To many churchgoers a feeling of inner peace, a sense of spiritual nourishment received, a sense of sin forgiven and iniquity taken away would typify their experience. A personal need has been met.

All these have a legitimate place, but to rest here is to stop short of the full cycle. The vision of Isaiah has always seemed to me to offer a perfect scheme for an act of worship. The sense of the presence of God - the consequent realization of sinfulness - the reception of forgiveness. But the sequel must not be omitted: the question is heard. 'Whom shall I send?' and the response is made, 'Here am I: send me.'

An act of worship is incomplete that does not end in a sense of mission. The words are there in the liturgy - or at least they are in Series II and III; but they need to be implemented. It is not enough that the light shines upon us: we must reflect it back into the world. 'Let your light so shine before men ... that they may glorify your Father which is in Heaven.'

My final image, then, is of a Church with the lights on inside and the light streaming out through its stained-glass, which is thus transformed to those without into something of beauty and meaning.

TIME FOR SILENCE?

'It is impossible nowadays to have a quiet time of prayer before a service, because members of the congregation come in and chat. No one seems to have any reverence. We go to church to worship God. The church is not a club.'

THE WORD 'club' suggests to me a rather stuffy place where people come in, grab *Punch* or *Country Life*, flop

into a leather chair and ignore everyone else. Let us hope
the Church is in no way like that.

What the Church is supposed to be is a fellowship. We
are ordered to love one another with a pure heart
fervently: we are officially compared to a body – to no less
than Christ's own Body – in which, if one member suffers,
the whole Body should suffer in sympathy: we are
commanded to 'rejoice with those that do rejoice and weep
with those that weep.' The earliest Christians were a
close-knit community: 'they met constantly to hear the
apostles preach and to share the common life, to break
bread and to pray. A sense of awe was everywhere.'

I very much doubt if this sense of awe depended on the
celebrant using archaic language, or having his back to the
congregation, or not being called by his Christian name
(why is it a *Christian* name if it is not to be used by
Christians?), or any of the things which you claim are
productive of awe. None of these things are either here or
there to me.

It is a sense of God we should hope to experience in
worship. Awe is only one facet of this. I have found the
sense of God overwhelmingly in services where there is a
strong element of Christian fellowship – where we do
express our mutual concern in the intercessions and are
aware of each other's joys and sorrows and problems. There
is a time for awe: there are other times when I could shout
for joy.

I can sympathize with your desire for silent prayer
before worship, but not with your irritation with those who
talk to each other after entering the church. If they are
getting up to date with the sort of information that could
make their prayers for each other meaningful, this is an
important part of their preparation for worship.

To call it irreverent is to put far too narrow a meaning
on that word. For some people it is almost confined to
tip-toeing about a church and talking in hushed voices. My
sympathies are with the little girl who concluded that God
was permanently asleep. True reverence to God must
include reverence to God's people.

But the two attitudes are not incompatible. If all those
partaking in a service were to meet first and get up to date
with each other's affairs, welcome any newcomers and *then*,
as a preliminary to the liturgy, *share* a few minutes
corporate silence, I believe that all would be the gainers.

KNEELING VERSUS STANDING

'Why are churchgoers increasingly encouraged to stand rather than kneel during the prayers? It is much easier to attend to one's devotions in a kneeling position with eyes closed than when standing, which is tiring for the aged and infirm.'

I SHOULD imagine that this is part of the modern attempt to recover a sense of the fellowship of the Holy Spirit. I find that kneeling, especially with my eyes shut, is an insulating position, whereas standing - I don't know why - has something corporate about it. It expresses solidarity.

How I would have loved to have been at that historic performance of the 'Messiah' when the congregation, led by the King, stood for the Hallelujah chorus. I know of no more moving expression of spontaneous respect than for everyone to rise to their feet. It is what you would do if the Queen were to enter the room. It is implicit in the phrase 'a standing ovation'.

It is of course impossible to be objective about physical posture. Why do we sit for the epistle and stand for the gospel? I often feel a strong urge to stand for one of the greater passages of the epistles.

But to pursue the comparison with Royalty further: you would stand at the entry of the Queen but you would kneel to receive honour, such as knighthood, from her. It is on this sort of ground that I would prefer kneeling for the reception of the Sacrament. But, if others wish to show corporate respect by standing, I am happy to stand with them.

Your point about eyes shut gets us on to more important ground. It suggests an attitude to God which I do not share. I find it easier to fix my thoughts on God, especially in meditation, by looking at something than by excluding vision. God is not absent from his creation but present in it. Supremely, we are taught, is he present in other people. An awareness of one's fellow-worshippers ought to be an aid to worship rather than a distraction.

I do, however, think it important not to be dogmatic about things like position. I shall always remember a woman who would not come to Communion because she had a stiff leg and was incapable of kneeling. Someone had driven it into her subconscious mind that it was 'irreverent' to receive the Sacrament not kneeling. It took me a long time to unscramble her inhibitions, and to help her see that reception of the Sacrament had the overriding priority and that there could be no possible irreverence in not kneeling if one was physically unable to. It is dangerous to form set habits in this sort of thing.

Finally, the aged and infirm are always entitled to adopt a posture more suited to their condition. In the Middle Ages congregations usually stood, but benches were provided round the walls for the elderly – hence, I suppose, the phrase, 'the weakest go to the wall.' There should be nothing humiliating about claiming your rights as a senior citizen.

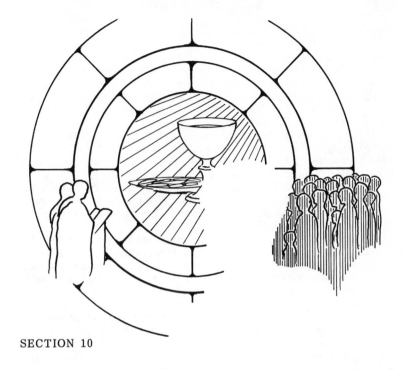

Liturgy

THE PRIEST OR THE PEOPLE?

*'The Church of England has still a lot to learn about full
congregational participation in worship.'*

I WISH I knew what you mean by 'full'. It seems to me that
there are two extremes to be avoided. One is the mumbling
of the whole service by the whole congregation; the other
is to have it recited entirely by the priest.

I do hope that people still read Evelyn Underhill, and
particularly her book entitled *Worship*. 'The corporate
service,' she says, '... the concerted action in which all
take a real part - is a more complete act of adoration, more
congenial to the Christian spirit and also more efficacious

for the common life.'

I think that common sense can safely be left to distinguish those parts of the liturgy which are appropriate to full and audible participation by the congregation from those which require a more professional expression. It is abundantly clear to me that the General Confession and the Creed gain by the former method, whereas the reading of the lessons demands the latter.

It is in some places only possible for the congregation to partake by means of its appointed representatives. I must safeguard the position that it is possible to be partaking *fully* while remaining silent.

To hear a lesson read really well is probably the best way to receive its message and to respond to it (and there is *no* need to be following the text in your own Bible as if the reader were inaudible).

To hear psalms really well sung is to be free to be wafted to a spiritual altitude that I certainly never reached when preoccupied with the problem of fitting oddly pointed words to a difficult chant (and why on earth do people indignantly claim a 'right' to add their own lamentable efforts to those of a cathedral choir?)

What I *do* reproach the writers of Church music with is their taking the word 'Amen' out of the mouth of the congregation. It should be precisely by saying 'Amen' that the worshippers show that they have identified themselves with the prayer offered by the professionals.

Whenever possible I think that an act of worship should be the work of a team, even if that only means two people; for it then expresses the nature of the Church as the Body of Christ, which exhibits diversity of gifts but the same Spirit.

PLEASURE ALONE

'People keep complaining to me that they don't enjoy Church services. Surely we don't go to Church to enjoy ourselves?'

'WE WEREN'T put on this earth to enjoy ourselves' was a very common phrase in my childhood, and certainly any complaint about the boredom of church services would have produced the phrase which you quote. It might be instructive to continue the list a little further. 'We don't engage in matrimony to enjoy ourselves,' for instance.

That statement is true in so far as it is taken as
meaning 'the purpose for which we engage in matrimony is
not our own enjoyment.' That would be to put a selfish
motive in the forefront. But it is also an absurd statement
because love simply doesn't think that way.

The next thing to say is that those who do not put
selfish motives first and who engage in matrimony for the
right reasons (which must include mutual love) do in fact
get a great deal of joy out of it, and if they do not get
this joy, then there must be something wrong with their
relationship.

With these considerations in mind, may we come back to
your question. Our *motive* for engaging in worship is most
certainly not our own enjoyment, and if we go to Church
with that end in mind we are certain to be disappointed.
Worship has very little entertainment value, except perhaps
in a cathedral, and then only for the tiny minority who
enjoy Church music.

But if you do really *engage* in worship – if you put God
in the very centre of your consciousness for just these fifty
or sixty minutes; if you listen to his Word and receive his
Gifts, if you allow him to cleanse your sin and confer on
you his forgiveness, if you respond to his love in willing
obedience to his commandment that we should love our
neighbours, so that the love of God leads naturally to the
Fellowship of the Holy Spirit – I don't see how you can fail
to come out of Church renewed in joy. And what else is
enjoyment?

I would not hesitate to add that, if you experience none
of these in the course of a service, there is something
deeply wrong with it as an act of worship. The wrong may
lie with those responsible for conducting it, or it may lie in
your own failure to make use of what the liturgy offers,
or, of course, it may be a combination of both.

COMPUTERIZED LITURGY?

'Is it possible to compile a satisfactory liturgy by computer?'

THERE IS one question which must be asked before this one
can be posed: should the words of a liturgy come from the
rank and file of worshippers, or from a person or persons
specially qualified to write them? Should liturgy be
expressive or suggestive? Should it take up what the

average worshipper brings with him to church, or should it impose some objective standard upon him?

These questions are not, of course, mutually exclusive. The answer could well be that a liturgy requires to be a bit of each. But it could only be produced by a computer if it were to be wholly expressive. A computer is not and never can be a creative artist.

So let us return to the question whether you want congregations to write their own liturgy or someone to write it for them.

I would myself urge that neither process is wholly satisfactory. The liturgies of the Church of England have been all of the latter type, and I think that they are all open to the criticism that they only too often fail to evoke a meaningful sense of worship in too many of the participants, which may be one reason why there are so few participants these days.

But I would not wish to transfer wholly to the other camp and to leave it entirely to congregations to 'throw up' their own formulas of worship which could then be averaged out by computer. I think that F.H. Brabant was right when he said, 'We cannot most of us express ourselves; unless we are geniuses we need the poet, the musician, the saint to do it for us. Poetry expresses what we could never have said, what perhaps we could never even have felt consciously unless it had been stirred up in us by the voice that has the key to our hearts.'

This is true as far as it goes, but it cannot be assumed that the writer of liturgy does have the key to all hearts; and the place of the computer seems to be to digest and tabulate the *response* of congregations to the suggestions of the liturgy-writer.

It has been argued that the saying, 'Only the best is good enough for God', applies to the words of the liturgy as much as to anything else. I think there is a misunderstanding here. Worship is not the offering of formulas to God. It is the offering of our hearts in penitence and praise and thanksgiving.

The best words are therefore not those which would gain the highest marks as literature or poetry, but those which would best evoke worship in the hearts of most worshippers. I do not see why a computer should not be able to assist us to assess which formula is the most effective.

NO MAGIC IN NEW SERVICES?

'The magic seems to have gone out of services these days.'

I AM going to take you seriously on this word 'magic'. The only technical use of the word in modern thought known to me is in R.G. Collingwood's *The Principles of Art*.

Here he distinguishes art proper from 'magic', which he defines as a process whereby emotions are aroused which are then discharged into the daily activities of life. He also distinguishes 'magic' from 'entertainment', which he calls 'a device for the discharge of emotions in such a way that they shall not interfere with the concerns of practical life.'

Thus a music critic might have unkind things to say about the National Anthem, and he might be right. But he would be judging as art something which ought to be judged as magic. The aim of a National Anthem is to arouse and nurture patriotic and loyalist emotions which will be discharged into our everyday living. If it succeeds in this, it is a good National Anthem.

With this definition of magic established, we might now consider in what sense worship is 'magic' and in what sense 'entertainment'. Insofar as worship is the ritual of a society and is designed to encourage its members to be proud of that society and to behave accordingly, it partakes of magic. Insofar as worship discharges the emotions which it generates within the act of worship – as perhaps in the penitential section – it partakes of 'entertainment'. The object of entertainment of this sort is to obtain what the Greeks called 'catharsis' or cleansing.

But the question must arise as to exactly which society is making the magic. With an established Church the rituals might well be a sub-division of the patriotic rituals – the rites of England seen as a 'Christian country'. They could be saying, 'God's in his Heaven, all's right with the world – or at any rate with that part of the world ruled from Westminster.'

But the magic of the Church of England could be subtly different from the magic of the Church of God. The emotions aroused could be different, and they could be discharged with different effect into your daily living.

It is possible that there is no magic in the worship of your church. But it is equally possible that those in charge are not trying to offer the magic that you are looking for, but a different sort of magic instead.

But it is also possible that you mean something totally different by 'magic'!

WHY THE 'PEACE'?

'Why is it particularly the Peace of the Lord that we are required to pass to each other in the new services?'

'PEACE' is a very big word. In the Hebrew it has the basic meaning of 'wholeness'. We can seek this both as an inner wholeness of personality and as an integration with other people, the forming of a larger whole which is a community. I am sure that the two go hand in hand – that we cannot and do not attain to inner wholeness except by seeking our proper place in the community.

The Greeks had a definition of education: 'out of many to become one.' If education is regarded – as it so largely is today – as the imparting of information that will be useful for the exercise of a profession, it is not very likely to achieve this aim.

But, although there is no inconsistency between the pursuit of inner wholeness and the pursuit of integration within a community, it needs to be stressed that our individuality is something to be prized. Martin Buber, a great authority on Jewish mysticism, makes this point when he says: 'Every man is unique, and his uniqueness is given to him that he may unfold it and make it flower ... Each person is a new thing in the world, and he should bring to perfection that which makes him unique.' But Buber goes on to say that this uniqueness 'is unfolded by his way of living with others.'

To see one's place in the community, to acknowledge that one is but a part of a greater whole, is the goundwork of humility. Buber sees humility as lying very close to compassion: 'the truly humble *feel* others as they feel themselves.'

To be proud is to be in competition; to be humble is to co-operate. For in competition we set our uniqueness over against the uniqueness of others, and in co-operation we offer our uniqueness to the service of others. The true community will value the importance of individuality. Not only is the humble man to cherish his own uniqueness; he must cherish that of everyone else. 'Every soul stands bright and clear before him in the splendour of its own existence.'

If this wholeness is the foundation of our peace – the peace which Jesus gives but which the world cannot give – then the formula, 'The Peace of the Lord be always with you,' is the richest blessing which we either desire for ourselves or confer upon others.

'PEACE' IS NOT A GIMMICK

'The "peace" seems to me to be just a gimmick and most undignified.'

IF YOU want to argue against something you must take it at its real best, not its imaginary worst.

Whenever I think about the Peace my mind goes to the improvised chapel in the oval vestibule of a beautiful country house which is used as a conference centre in the diocese of Salisbury. The occasion is the meeting of a number of curates for in-service training.

For three days we have been living together, praying together, reading together, laughing together, discussing together; problems and frustrations have been shared; steam has been let off about the intransigent 'boss' or the stuffy parishioner. A very real level of fellowship has been established.

And now we come to the final Eucharist in that stately stone hall. Its oval shape is matched by a ring of chairs. The table which we use for an altar is still the focal point, but we can all see each other as well.

Intercession is offered in the form of spontaneous prayer, each contributing as he feels moved. By now we know each other well enough for this to flow naturally, and together we offer our deepest concerns to God. The Confession. The Absolution and the wonderful sense of liberation that comes with it. The Prayer of Humble Access.

Now we are ready to approach the climax to our act of worship. We had started by praying that we 'may perfectly love you.' The thought comes back: *if you love me, you will keep my commandments*. What is it that he commands? *A new commandment I give you, that you love one another*.

We stand for the Peace. I approach the man who is nearest to me. Hands join and eyes meet. 'The Peace of the Lord be always with you, dear Matthew.' The pressure of the hands tightens perceptibly: 'and also with you, dear

Ian.' This is the real thing - the love of God and the fellowship of the Holy Spirit. This is authentic encounter with God. *If we love one another, God dwelleth in us.*

I pass to the next man. Relations have not been quite so good here: but, if there is anything amiss between us, it could not possibly survive this moment. 'The Peace of the Lord be always with you, *dear* Mark' - and I mean that 'dear' as I have never meant it before. Meanwhile the others are greeting each other in the same way.

Undignified? I repudiate the word. In Latin *dignus* means 'worthy'. How *could* love and sincerity of this sort be unworthy of him who commanded it? We are now ready to receive the Sacrament. *He that loveth not his brother whom he hath seen, how can he love God whom he hath not seen?* We do - so we can.

PUTTING ON A NEW NATURE

'Passing the Peace: "as to embracing and looking into each others' eyes which might cause some people to have feelings and thoughts of lust and sex - how terrible."'

YOUR LETTER makes sorry reading. 'To the pure all things are pure.' Am I to understand that there are so-called Christians in our Communions who dare not look each other in the eyes and clasp each other by the hand for fear of lustful and lascivious thoughts? I hope you do them an injustice. I might add that there is a kind of vicarious lust which consists in wondering if other people are having lascivious thoughts.

You say of St Paul: 'Any gesture likely to cause wrong feelings would have been farthest from his mind.' Let us look at what St Paul did say. He urged Christians to greet each other with a holy kiss. If this were wrong within the liturgy because it excited lustful thoughts, it would be just as wrong outside the context of the liturgy.

Of course St Paul 'tells of the immoral times of his day.' He does so in Colossians 3:5 - 'fornication, indecency, lust, foul cravings and the ruthless greed that is nothing less than idolatry'. But how does he go on? Verse 9: 'You have discarded the old nature with its deeds and put on a new nature which is being constantly renewed in the image of its Creator.'

And what is this *new nature*? Verse 12: 'the garments

that suit God's chosen people, his own, his beloved:
compassion, kindness, humility, gentleness, patience. Be
forbearing with one another, and forgiving where any have
cause for complaint: you must forgive as the Lord forgave
you.'

This is where the Kiss of Peace came in, in the liturgies
of the early Church. They do not seem to have been afraid
of lust rearing its ugly head, because they knew that they
had passed from darkness to light.

There is a lot about the Peace in Gregory Dix's *Shape of
the Liturgy*. It was, he says, the liturgical expression of
the words in Matthew 5:23. 'If, when you are bringing your
gift to the altar, you suddenly remember that your brother
has a grievance against you ... first go and make peace
with your brother, and only then come and offer your gift.'
In the third century the deacon introduced the Peace with
the words: 'Is there any man keepeth aught against his
brother?' It was not thought right to receive Communion in
the absence of fellowship.

Dix describes the Peace as 'the symbol of that fellowship
of the Holy Ghost of which the "communion" of the Church
is only the consequence and the outward sign'; and again
as 'a striking instance ... of the way in which the liturgy
was regarded as a solemn putting into act before God of the
whole Christian living of the Church's members.' If they
could do it, why cannot we?

GESTURE OF LOVE

*'Why do we so seldom see the "Pax" at the Eucharist being
enacted with gestures instead of just words?'*

IT WOULD not be going too far to say that I have found in
the Pax a new dimension to worship and a new reality to
Christian fellowship. But I must add that I have chiefly
experienced it in such non-parochial situations as retreats
and residentiary courses. In these there has always been
an already existing element of community which is at the
same time expressed and nourished by the Pax.

It is this balance between the expressive and the
creative or nutritive role which seems to me to be the
important one. I have heard of parishes which have tried to
introduce the practice and have abandoned it because it
seemed hypocritical. I take this to mean that it seemed to

be presupposing a level of fellowship which did not, in fact, exist. I wonder whether, with a little perseverance, they might not have created thereby the very fellowship which they lacked.

Whether worshippers who have, and are content to have, so little sense of Christian fellowship have any right to be sharing Holy Communion is another question.

But I wonder if there is not another nettle to be grasped of a more subtle nature. I would locate the sting of this nettle in the fact that while we have, as Christians, the most urgent and authoritative mandate to love each other, we can seldom, in a non-erotic situation, *say* that we love each other.

How embarrassed would you be if another member of the congregation, or one of your clergy, said to you (and without any husky urgency of the voice or gentle pressure on the knee): 'I love you'?

I remember once enquiring of a public school chaplain after two boys in his school and receiving the answer: 'I love them.' I did not and do not doubt the integrity of that chaplain, but I thought him very brave to use that phrase. For a great many people, I think, the erotic overtones of 'I love you' would be insuperable. But, if you can't say it with words – say it with something else. Say it with that clasp of the hands and that look in the eye which is, I think, the best form of gesture to accompany the words.

For those who would find, in even this element of physical contact, unacceptable erotic overtones I can only feel deeply sorry. Those who were brought up by people who were afraid of sex, who have been moulded by a society whose attitude to sex is cock-eyed, must not be blamed for their inhibitions or forced to act as if these were not real. But it is the mark of the true believer that he can handle dangerous things (metaphorical snakes?) with impunity.

I believe that in any truly Christian community the Pax would take its place simply and naturally as the means of expressing and of building up our Christian love.

N.B. I have devoted a lot of space to this subject because, as I say in my Introduction, this is the one on which I have received the largest number of questions.

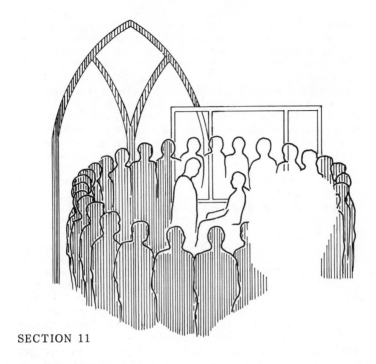

Eucharist

WHY NOT MATTINS?

'Why do the clergy seem so keen to offer us Communion all the time and to deprive us of Mattins? Is there something wrong with Mattins?'

THERE IS nothing wrong with Mattins at all. It is a very good form of service.

The *Venite* is a wonderful introduction to an act of worship; the *Te Deum* is a tremendous outburst of praise and adoration; so is the *Jubilate*. The psalms and lessons offer a solid base of biblical religion; the third collect is a lovely daily prayer. Those who have denigrated Mattins in order to enhance the idea of a Parish Communion have done us a disservice.

But you seem to be proposing Mattins as an alternative to Holy Communion. It was meant to be the preface. Your complaint that 'too much Holy Communion causes indigestion' makes no sense to me at all, especially since you seem to think that once a week is too frequent for its celebration.

The fact that Mattins is an excellent form of service in no way detracts from the fact that Holy Communion is the central act of Christian worship and the only one that can claim its origins in Jesus Christ himself. It has an element of commitment in it which is not necessarily present in Mattins or Evensong. The value of these is that they provide an act of worship for those who are not yet ready for this commitment.

The promoters of Parish Communion have done well to re-assert the *primacy* of the Eucharist in our scheme of worship. This should be the service at which we pull out all the stops, at which the choir contributes the dimension of music and the preacher expounds the Word of God. It should be noted that, in the Prayer Book, Holy Communion is the only service which makes specific provision for a sermon.

I have never been able to accept any criterion for the frequency of Communion; that is why I stated that it should have *primacy* in our scheme of worship. To confine it to a said celebration at an early hour or to tack it on as an optional extra to Mattins, is hardly to give it primacy.

Anyone can 'cheapen' Holy Communion as often as he likes by failure to take it seriously or to prepare for it intelligently. But people will not necessarily take it any more seriously if it is offered less frequently.

I would have thought this an admirable subject for discussion by a PCC or by some wider meeting of the congregation.

AT HOME OR IN CHURCH

'What do you think are the pros and cons of House Communion as opposed to a celebration in Church?'

I CANNOT see any need to choose between them: they are probably best thought of as complementary to each other.

Those who have experienced House Communion often experience an impact and a sense of involvement which they easily miss in a Church service. There is a compactness and an intimacy which enables the celebrant to use the quiet voice of sincerity. It is sometimes difficult for a priest, concentrating on voice production up at the other end of a large church, to feel that he is worshipping with his congregation at all.

These, too, may find in the very absence of ecclesiastical architecture and liturgical formality an aid to relevance and participation. Words that are normally sung can spring to new significance through being said. Formulas that have degenerated into formalities can break through and become meaningful through being used in a living room. The mere fact that worship is taking place in the scene of one's daily life can forge the vital link between worship and living. A religion that is thus expressed can hardly be pigeon-holed as 'something that happens on Sunday'.

But I do not mean by this to discount the value of worship in a church. Where any large numbers are concerned this is a matter of mere practical necessity. It also offers the opportunity of external aids.

By this I mean such influence upon the mind or mood as music, ceremonial or architecture can produce. Music, as my uncle Bishop Colin Dunlop used to say, 'is the very language of ecstasy.' It is the most ethereal of the arts and can take us, in worship, far beyond the point where words fail. It can also reduce an act of worship to the status of a concert.

Ceremonial - the use of bodily movement, sometimes enhanced and sometimes circumscribed by the wearing of colourful, majestic or symbolic clothing - can be a means towards an end which is worship. It can also degenerate into a fetish which is an end in itself.

Architecture may create the mood for worship. Cathedrals, as Joseph Addison observed, 'by opening the mind to vast conceptions, fit it for the reception of the Deity.' But they can also provide an experience which is merely aesthetic and therefore a distraction. But once the danger of distraction is recognized and faced, the fact is that music, ceremonial and architecture can be so used as to be of great assistance to the would-be worshipper, by making an act of worship a complex offering of all that is best in man's attainment to the glory of God.

N.B. It might be useful to underline the distinction between house Communion and house Churches.

WHITE WINE OR RED?

'Why do we now have white wine instead of red for Holy Communion? In view of Christ's own words, 'my blood', I find this change most distressing, if not a heresy.'

I WONDER whom you mean by 'we'? I have frequently come across the use of white wine in England and never had anything else on the Continent. There has been no change of policy – indeed there is no policy to change, nor can there be any question of heresy.

It does not make the slightest difference if the wine is red, white or rosé. If God can turn red wine into 'the blood of Christ', he can most certainly turn white wine also. There is no reason that I can see why the consecrated wine should resemble the *colour* of blood. It does not taste like blood nor smell like blood (for both of which we may be thankful), nor has it any other properties of blood.

It must have been this sort of approach that led to the medieval doctrine of transubstantiation. These properties such as colour, smell and taste were known then as 'accidents.' It is not a very useful term today and can be misleading. But the Church held that in the act of consecration, the 'accidents' remained unchanged but the 'substance' – an even more misleading word today – was changed. It *was* heresy not to believe that, and you could be burned alive for professing the contrary.

I think that the best attempt to replace 'transubstantiation' by a term which is intelligible today is in the word 'transvaluation'. It does not alter the doctrine, so far as I can see, but it makes use of a concept with which we are familiar.

A piece of paper that has passed through the Mint becomes a pound note. It is still paper – its 'accidents' are unchanged (except by the addition of printer's ink) – but its value has been most significantly changed. While remaining paper it has *become* money. Its essential nature – which used to be called its 'substance' – has been changed.

I think that your question is rather like suggesting that a pound note ought to be printed on silver paper!

I think that the purpose of this doctrine is to prevent people from trying to take our Lord's words, 'This is my blood,' literally. To do so is to rob them of their significance. Drinking actual blood is merely revolting, especially to a Jew, and quite meaningless. It is only when taken metaphorically that the words make sense, for this enables us to pack into the word 'blood' the significance which it acquired in Hebrew thinking through its use in sacrifice.

SHARING THE SACRAMENT

'It has been stated that two people who do not agree about the 'Real Presence' ought not to share the Sacrament. Why on earth not?'

WE ARE UP against the curious phenomenon of historical memory here, for this was the sort of thing the Protestants used to be burned alive for not believing. Arguments on the subject still engender heat.

I have on several occasions in my column in the Press drawn attention to the relationship between believing and understanding. The doctrine of the Real Presence gives me a good example of what I mean.

I think that no Christian can do less than take the texts seriously and honestly. There is nothing dishonest about taking our Lord's words metaphorically, as we are bound to take the statement 'I am the true Vine' metaphorically and symbolically. Thus, just as a campaigning author might hold up his pen to a soldier and say, 'This is *my* sword,' so Jesus may be taken as saying to the believer in Jewish sacrifice, 'This is *my* means of reconciling God and Man.' That would be a sensible metaphorical interpretation of 'This is my blood.'

But the St John texts are unequivocal in claiming for the bread-become-'flesh' a very definite power. Through these means Jesus dwells in the hearts of his worshippers and his eternal life becomes theirs.

I can believe all this because I can understand it, and I like William Temple's word 'transvaluation' for this reason. The idea of food doing something to the consumer is perfectly easy to grasp. That Jesus is *active through* the Sacrament I *can* understand. But, when I am told that he is *present in* the bread – this is something to which I can put no content.

It is not a question of whether I *believe* it; I merely cannot understand it; the idea of a person being 'present' in a piece of bread relates to nothing in my experience. But, if a Roman Catholic or an Anglo-Catholic is able to put

any content to such a proposition, the best of British luck
to him. I am perfectly happy to kneel and receive alongside
him, though I cannot share his belief at present.

I add the words 'at present' because it seems quite
possible that some experience will come my way, or some
explanation be offered, which will enable me to understand
and share his belief. Pending such an event, he will
probably think me irreverent because I cannot without
hypocrisy offer reverence *to* a sacrament.

To me the *process* is the significant thing, and I can
receive the Sacrament with a great sense of joy and
humility, which are to me the essential elements of
reverence. But I cannot see on what grounds anyone could
be justified in refusing to receive Communion alongside
someone who holds my views.

BY ANY OTHER NAME ...

*'Should Anglicans use the word "Mass" to describe Holy
Communion?'*

OF COURSE *Mass* is a controversial word, and there is
always a good case to be made out for dropping
controversial words in the interests of the peace of God.

To some the word *Mass* can relight the fires of
Smithfield. To those who wish to emphasize the break with
Rome and all the perversions of the Middle Ages, the word
is simply anathema. Equally, for those who wish to stress
the element of continuity between the Church of England
and its historic past, the word is often favoured. It would
be a worthwhile exercise for many of us to try and put
these controversial thoughts and inflamed feelings out of
our minds, and to look at this issue on its own intrinsic
merits.

I was always taught that the word *Mass* derives from the
dismissal at the end of the service, *Ite, missa est,* which
comes out again in our English liturgy as 'Go in peace and
serve the Lord.'

If your choice is not dictated by churchmanship
prejudice, you have three main alternatives: *Holy
Communion*, *Eucharist* and *Mass*. They each emphasize a
different aspect of the service.

Communion stresses the fellowship with God and with the
other worshippers which ought to find expression and

nourishment in the liturgy. Obviously this name has a very serious claim on our attention.

Eucharist focuses on the act of consecration. Jesus Christ consecrated by giving thanks. I see an appeal here also to live eucharistically, consecrating, instead of refusing, 'everything created by God'. This word also has an important claim.

At first sight the word *Mass* – dismissal – can hardly presume to stand equal to these, which describe the essential meaning of the act. But, on deeper reflection, a case can certainly be made out for it.

William Temple laid down the principle that the position of Christianity is not that conduct is all-important and that prayer helps conduct, but that prayer is all-important and that conduct *tests* prayer. I think it is a legitimate extension of that principle to say: for prayer read worship.

Our relationship with God is what matters, and worship is primarily concerned with this. But, if you have really got into relationship with God, then your conduct after you leave church will be profoundly affected. Conversely, if we go out into the world and continue to behave in a sub-Christian manner, who can dare to say we have been in touch with the living God?

Missa is close to the word 'mission'. If *Mass* means a reminder of the mission of the whole Church, it stands for something important. Choose which you like, but choose in charity. We should not be quarrelling about such trifles.

SACRIFICIAL RITE?

'Is it true to say that the Eucharist is a sacrifice?'

I CANNOT see any point in answering this question until we are agreed on what we mean by sacrifice. I believe it to be a subject on which there is considerable misunderstanding. Again and again I have found that, when people say they do not believe this or that doctrine, what is really true is that they do not understand it.

St Augustine says, in the *City of God*: 'Sacrifice is every deed that is done to the end that we cleave to God in fellowship.' It is a very wide interpretation, but, if we consider such phrases as 'the sacrifice of God is a troubled spirit; a broken and contrite heart, O God wilt thou not despise' or 'this our sacrifice of praise and thanksgiving' –

we shall soon need a definition as wide as Augustine's.

Sin is a barrier between man and God and an impediment to fellowship. It is often removed by a contrite heart; contrition therefore helps us to cleave to God in fellowship. Praise and thanksgiving also help to achieve this end.

That the Eucharist only makes sense *in terms* of sacrifice seems to me to be beyond argument. A little girl asked on being taken up to the alter-rail for a blessing: 'Mummy, was that really blood you were drinking?' A crudely literal interpretation of 'This is my Blood' is merely revolting. Unless it is given the sense of the blood of sacrifice it is bound to be so.

I am not competent to speak for either extreme of the churchmanship spectrum, but I have always understood that the 'Protestant' objection to the idea that the Eucharist *is* a sacrifice is held to impugn the all-sufficiency of Christ's sacrifice upon the Cross.

I have never had the 'Catholic' argument put to me in terms which I have understood. Too often the speaker has been more at pains to defend the doctrine than to explain it. But I have a phrase from Michael Ramsey which I find both intelligible and satisfying: 'Christ offers the perfect sacrifice which mankind was incapable of offering, so that now – cleansed by his blood and incorporated into him – we may offer ourselves to him.'

Two more phrases from Augustine come to mind in this context. 'He willed that we ourselves should be his sacrifice' and 'This is the Christian sacrifice: the many become one Body in Christ.' Incorporation into Christ involves organic connection with other members of the body, and in the fellowship of the Holy Spirit – once again – we 'cleave to God'.

AN UNHYGIENIC PRACTICE?

'Is it not unhygienic and rather revolting to share the chalice at Communion?'

THERE WAS, some time ago, a prolonged correspondence in *The Times* on this subject which was, I thought, inconclusive. It did, however, show that there are two distinct issues: the question of infection and the question of squeamishness.

On the subject of infection it seemed that the more

qualified correspondents made three points which are
important. One was that germs undoubtedly are deposited
on the chalice and could therefore be picked up from it.
The second was that the risk can be diminished by as much
as ninety per cent if the chalice is carefully wiped: if the
celebrant rotates the chalice, this may only be needed once
for every altar-rail. The third point was that, although
there is abundant evidence that disease *could* be passed on
by this means, there is virtually none that it ever *is*. The
fact must be borne in mind that the great majority of
Anglicans find no insuperable obstacle here.

It goes, I hope, without saying that, if anyone knows he
has an infection, he should either communicate last or ask
to receive by intinction. It was, of course, suggested by
some correspondents that intinction should be the norm.
There is a practical difficulty in that it really requires
three hands to accomplish it, but with more than one
assistant it should not be impossible.

But some would oppose here that they see a positive
symbolism in the sharing of the cup, and here we come up
against the question of squeamishness.

If I were in a restaurant and were served a drink in a
cup or a glass which had evidently not been washed since
it was last used, I would be extremely reluctant to drink
from it. For those whose natural revulsion here is strong it
would be an act of grossest irreverence to import such
conditions and emotions into the reception of the Sacrament.
It is bound to be a matter of individual taste, and I can
only say that, whereas I am myself rather inclined to
squeamishness of this sort, I am perfectly satisfied by the
careful wiping of the chalice with a purificator.

I have to add, however, that there seems to be a
connection between squeamishness, or lack of
squeamishness, and love. I am far more ready to share a
cup or a glass with my wife, or with a close friend, than
with an unknown stranger. There are also those who would
regard it as in some way 'irreverent' to wipe the
consecrated wine off the chalice at all; but to me this would
imply some crudely literalistic interpretation of the words,
'This is my blood'.

*N.B. This subject has come into new prominence since the
scare about AIDS. The recent correspondence leads me to
underline the point about those who think they are carry-
ing an infection taking the appropriate steps.*

DIGNITY OF HUMAN HANDS

'Why do some people refuse to receive Communion into their hands?'

IT IS, of course, in the rubrics of the Book of Common Prayer that communicants should receive 'into their hands', and this should certainly be regarded as the normal practice of Anglicans. How important it is is a matter of opinion.

I have myself only once asked someone why she preferred to receive direct to her lips, and I got the answer that it was irreverent to touch the sacrament with 'unclean hands' – unclean being clearly understood in a merely ritual and symbolic sense.

I cannot see any force in this argument at all. We do not sin with our hands: we sin with our imaginations. If you insist on passing the responsibility for sin on to other, more palpable portions of the anatomy, I would have thought that lips were as likely to be 'unclean' as hands. They are certainly more often the instruments of the sinful imagination, especially among the sort of people who are likely to be communicants and are seldom guilty of murder, violence or theft.

I would like to plead, while I am at it, for the dignity of human hands. Most great portrait-painters take as much care with the hands as with the face. For these, too, can be tellingly expressive of personality – ranging from the fine, sensitive fingers of the artist or musician to the more rough-hewn grandeur of the hands of the manual labourer or craftsman.

Then think also of how we use our hands in human relationships. The instinctive gesture of the child in search of confidence is to slip his hand into that of an adult. Our hands provide the obvious gesture of fellowship and can convey the deepest messages of sympathy. And, when it comes to love, is it not through the hands that the first vibrant message is communicated? John Donne puts it quite beautifully in his poem, *The Exstasie*:

> *So to intergraft our hands was yet*
> *The only means to make us one.*

But the last word is with the sculptor Rodin, whose strangely moving group representing two right hands, fingertip groping delicately towards fingertip, is so delightfully suggestive of hearts that are open to the stimulus of other hearts. He called it *La Cathédrale*, and it only takes a little sympathetic imagination to see why.

For a cathedral is in some respects only a church writ large, and it is good to think of a church as a place where all that we do with our hands - our work, our art, our music, our gestures of comfort and sympathy and love - are consecrated to God. How better can we consecrate them than by holding them out to receive him in the bread and the wine of Communion?

SHOULD I LOOK AT THE CELEBRANT?

'I was always taught not to look at the celebrant when receiving Communion; but I notice that many people do, and wonder if this is right.'

YOU REMIND ME of a little girl in a family who has been told not to 'look' during Family Prayers and who suddenly said: 'I can see someone who is looking.' But we will forget about that.

If I were asked where I thought the chief failure of the Church lay I would give very serious consideration to the possible answer, 'in failure to realize - to make real - the fellowship of the Holy Spirit.' I do not mean that there has been total failure, but that there has been widespread and grievous failure.

As I have argued before, I incline to the opinion that the phrase 'the Communion of Saints' is best translated 'having in common holy things'. That partaking together in the Holy Communion *should* form a real and precious bond between all who do so seems to me to be beyond question. That it seldom does anything of the sort is a matter of experience.

I suspect that a great many churchgoers have been trained in habits of individual piety which must make the linking of *communion with each other* and *communion with God* extremely difficult. I have had letters objecting to the enactment of the Peace ... 'it causes distraction at a point in the service which should be calm, still and peaceful with all attention centred on the altar.' It is clear also that many people find prayer impossible if any awareness of other people (usually described as 'fidgeting') intrudes upon their consciousness.

It seems to me that this attitude forces too great a separation between what are to me inseparables – love for God and love for each other. I have a far more vivid experience of *God* in a Communion service where the element of human fellowship is conspicuous. This is usually in such contexts as residential conferences, post-ordination training meetings and so on, where there is an already existent fellowship to express which is, in turn, greatly enhanced by means of the Eucharist.

I would therefore welcome anything that fosters this feeling that, because we share in the Holy Spirit and in the holy things, we are *ipso facto* involved in a sharing with each other. I have lovely moments at the altar-rail with children who are brought up – my own usually manage to kiss me across the rail – and there is a sort of look which I find myself exchanging with some communicants in which there is a whole world of mutual understanding and fellowship. I cannot agree that this could ever be anything but right.

Bible

IGNORANCE OF THE O.T.

*'Is a full grounding in the Christian faith being given when,
in a growing number of Anglican churches, the Old
Testament has become a closed book?'*

YOU HAVE put your finger on what I regard as a very real
difficulty, but I believe that the problem is deeper than
you suggest. Even if the Old Testament lessons *were* read
regularly at your Eucharist, and even if there *was*
Evensong, could you really claim that your congregation
was receiving a 'full grounding' in the Christian faith?

The amount of real instruction that can be given in the
context of an act of worship is strictly limited. It is as far

from an ideal teaching situation as you could get.

The presence of young children is one of the limiting factors. A congregation often offers a very wide age-range, large numbers, and no opportunity for questions or discussion. Any teacher will tell you that the conditions requisite for giving instruction are a narrow age-range, small numbers, and good opportunities for questions and discussion.

The insertion of a thin slice of Old Testament – often of necessity without comment – into our worship is not going to take us very far along the way to being properly instructed. It does seem to me that the case for solid instruction in the Christian faith on a weekday in circumstances uninhibited by the context of worship is extremely strong.

Having said that, I fully agree with you that it would be a catastrophic loss if members of the Church of England were to be brought up in virtual ignorance of the Old Testament.

It has, of course, its own value. It is the record of the religious education of a particular race, and the insights and lessons derived from it are often directly relevant. The first chapter of Isaiah has still much to teach us. Many of the psalms are of eternal value as aids to prayer and meditation.

But I suppose that the main importance of the Old Testament is as the indispensable background against which to understand the New. As Bishop Gore said: 'Jesus Christ takes the Old Testament revelation for granted as God-given.'

Many of the central ideas of the Eucharist, for instance, are at best meaningless and at worst misleading without their background of Old Testament thought. The 'Lamb of God' could only be a piece of bleating sentimentality; the phrases, 'this is my body ... this is my blood', are merely revolting and cannibalistic unless we see behind them the Old Testament conception of sacrifice.

N.B. There are many books to be recommended on this subject. E. Charpentier: How to Read the Old Testament *is excellent. For a fuller treatment B.W. Anderson:* The Living World of the Old Testament.

WORD OF THE LORD?

*'Why did the compilers of the ASB use the passage from
Numbers 15: 22–36 for the 7th Sunday before Easter? ...
The problem is made more intense by hearing that "this
is the word of the Lord."'*

YOU ARE perfectly entitled to think as you do. I, of
course, cannot answer for the compilers of the ASB. But
you raise the whole question of the 'un-Christian' teaching
of parts of the Old Testament and those verses of the
psalms now printed in brackets.

I agree with you that the versicle, 'This is the word of
the Lord,' often sticks in one's throat. Many clergymen
whom I know and respect find themselves unable to use that
formula. I think that it is too prone to misunderstanding. I
fear that it must imply to many: 'This is valid religious
teaching for today.' But, if we try to take the view that
any command claimed by the Bible as coming from God must
be taken as a commandment to be obeyed today, we are in
trouble.

As I have pointed out before in my writing, the Old
Testament says, 'Thou *shalt* kill,' much more often than it
says, 'Thou shalt *not* kill.' We have to use our own
consciences, formed by *Christian* (as opposed to Judaistic)
teaching and practice, to judge between them. The Bible is
not a book of oracles; it is the record of the growth of the
understanding of God by a certain people. The more
primitive stages in that growth are no longer binding upon
us. I don't believe that even the most ardent of
fundamentalists would disagree with me and require us to
put these commands into practice.

Just to give you the full horror of this particular
situation I will quote an account from the *Daily Express* of
February 11, 1958, reprinted in a book called *Eye-witness.*
It describes a woman being stoned to death in Jeddah
according to Koranic law.

First she received a flogging of a hundred strokes
across the shoulders. 'Next, a lorry loaded with rocks and
stones was backed up and its cargo deposited in a pile. At
a signal from the prince (who was judge) the crowd leaped
on the stones and started pelting the woman to death.' In
the background an Air Line travel poster offered the
invitation: 'Come to the Middle East. Savour its romance,
its colour, its quaint traditions.' This one was hardly

quaint. 'The men snarled and shouted as they flung their
stones, their faces transformed into masks of sadism.' It
took just over an hour before the doctor pronounced the
woman dead.

'And the Lord said to Moses ... All the congregation
shall stone him with stones.' Perhaps your vicar would have
been wise to have preached on the topic. I can only
suppose that the compilers of the ASB wished to bring out
the contrast between this ghastly form of execution and Our
Lord's refusal to countenance its infliction on the woman
taken in adultery.

ANCIENT & MODERN

*'How should we decide which translation of the Bible to use
in church?'*

LET US first try to make up our minds on what is the
purpose of reading passages from Scripture aloud in a
service.

Is it a Bible-study period that aims to convey to
worshippers the full meaning of the text? Or is it, for want
of a better phrase, a ceremonial incantation where the
overtones conveyed by prose rhythms and the sequence of
vowel sounds are important and the exact understanding
pre-supposed? If it is the latter, there ought to be some
other occasion offered for Bible-study.

I have recently been preparing the lessons by comparing
the New English Bible with the Greek. Having done so, I
would often prefer the Authorised Version to be read in
church. But how many are willing to do such preparation?

To give an example. In Ephesians 1:4, the NEB gives:
'In Christ he chose us ... to be *dedicated*'. The Greek
word is 'hagios', for which the AV gives 'holy'. Now the
word 'holy' is charged with overtones which make it much
more suitable for what I have called 'ceremonial incantation'.
Can you imagine the *Sanctus* being sung (or even said)
'Dedicated, Dedicated, Dedicated, Lord God of Hosts'?

But, on the other hand, how many worshippers really
understand the word 'holy'? Does it convey more than a
vague sense of religiosity? I believe that the average
Anglican would be embarrassed if you called him holy and
urged him to become more holy. I would fancy my chances
higher if I were trying to persuade him to be more

dedicated.

A great deal of the epistles (or should I say 'letters'?) are not suitable for incantation. Apart from a few lyrical passages, St Paul did not write fine, resounding prose. He was hammering out an argument. Do you prefer, for Ephesians 1:8, 'wherein he hath abounded toward us in all wisdom and prudence', to the NEB paraphrase, 'Therein lies the richness of God's free grace lavished upon us, imparting full wisdom and insight'? Let no one say that this is 'supermarket' language, or even pedestrian. I certainly prefer it.

On the other hand, in Romans 12:15, 'with the joyful be joyful and mourn with the mourners' falls flat. 'Rejoice with them that do rejoice and weep with them that weep' is perfectly clear in its meaning, but offers a poetic rhythm which makes it memorable.

Look also at the Christmas gospel: 'When all things began the word already was.' That is even flatter. Is it more intelligible than 'In the beginning was the Word'? I find it impossible to use anything but the Authorised Version.

TOO MANY BIBLE VERSIONS?

'Do the scholars who keep producing new translations of the Bible realize what confusion they cause to simple believers?'

I DO NOT think it fair to describe the offer of a wide choice as *confusion*. It is something which can be put to good effect.

I have found that it offers a useful approach to Bible-study. I ask the group members to bring as wide a range of translations as possible; we note their discrepancies and try to see what each is getting at. It is not indispensable for the leader of such a group to know Greek, but he must have access to the commentaries.

Take a passage like the Sermon on the Mount. It does not provide, as many think, a simple religion uncluttered by the theologising of St Paul. But it is extremely familiar, not to say hackneyed. It is lyrical in style, and there are strong arguments for favouring the Authorised Version. It has passed into the deposit of English civilization. The portion of it set for Trinity 15 merits twelve entries in the *Oxford Dictionary of Quotations*.

Readers of Jane Austen will remember from *Mansfield Park* the words of Mr Crawford: 'Shakespeare one gets acquainted with without knowing how. It is part of an Englishman's constitution.' So, in former days, was the Authorised Version. Whether that status is of much religious value is open to question, but the fact remains that the AV text enshrines some notable errors.

The phrase, 'Take no thought for ...', is not only a bad translation: it is bad advice. Prudence has long been recognized as a Christian virtue. The Greek word means 'do not be anxious for ...' Let us say so.

To add 'one cubit to one's stature' is something that only a dwarf or a midget is likely to desire. To achieve it would make me over eight feet tall, and then I would have cause to be anxious about raiment. But the word translated 'stature' has the primary meaning of one's age or term of life; the word for 'cubit' can also mean a measure of time. Thus translated, the command makes sense. But it only appears as a footnote alternative in the New English Bible.

The NEB is not above criticism either. Are we really to admire the lilies because 'they do not work'? The root meaning of *kopiao* is 'to grow weary'. This is exactly expressed in the AV by 'they toil not.' Why change it? If this sort of process leads people into a deeper understanding of a passage which may have been assimilated with all its errors into the English way of life without any thought or criticism, then the diversity of translations seems to me to provide a healthy opportunity.

RSV THE BEST

'With regard to "loving use of the King James Bible" - surely the Revised Standard Version has all King James's English and sentence-construction without the archaic words and with the accuracy of a new translation.'

THAT IS certainly the compilers' claim. They state in their preface that they are glad to say with the King James translators: 'truly we never thought ... that we should need to make a new translation nor yet make of a bad one a good one ... but to make a good one better.'

Nevertheless, there has been strong opposition to any revision of the King James text right from the start. To some people it is faultless. In 1853 Frederick Faber claimed,

in a rather purple passage, that its language 'lives on in
the ear like music that never can be forgotten ... it is part
of the national mind and the anchor of the national
seriousness.' But already scholarship was bringing to light
earlier and more authentic versions of the Greek text than
those used by King James's translators.

When the first discoveries of the critics were heard,
Ruskin hurried to the defence of the old text:

Throw thou no shadow on the sacred page
Whose faults, if faults, are sanctified by age.

The idea that faults can be sanctified by age is not a little
sentimental. To those outside the faith this new evidence of
error was a powerful stick with which to beat the Church.

The authorities had a difficult choice between intellectual
honesty and pastoral expediency, for Bishop Christopher
Wordworth warned them: 'Beware that, by altering the text
of the authorised version of the Bible, you shake the faith
of many.' This does underline the precariousness of a faith
that is *founded* on any particular cultural expression of
Christianity. There is only one true foundation to faith,
and that is Jesus Christ himself.

In 1870 a committee was set up by Convocation under the
chairmanship of Bishop Ellicott. Although they were on the
whole conservative, they felt obliged to make 36,000
alterations. Some of these seem pointless. Why, for
instance, should the penitent *thief* have to become a
penitent *robber*?

Some questions of translation are not really soluble.
Christians still divide on largely, if not wholly,
un-theological grounds between those who prefer 'charity'
and those who prefer 'love' in I Corinthians 13 - though no
one has, to my knowledge, suggested the revision, 'the
King of charity my shepherd is.' Many new translations
were recognizable improvements, such as 'be not anxious'
for 'take no thought'.

Words do alter their meanings with time, and there is no
gain in retaining 'conversation' when we mean 'conduct', or
'communicate' when we mean 'share.'

*N.B. There is an excellent little introduction by C.S. Lewis
to J.B. Phillips' Letters to Young Churches which puts the
case for modern translation.*

CHURCH BEFORE THE WORD?

*'It is often said that the Church came before the Bible.
Surely the statement is wrong and even sinister, putting
the Church before the Word?'*

I SIMPLY cannot imagine what you mean by 'sinister'. As a
simple matter of historical fact the Church *did* exist before
any of the writings of the New Testament.

Jesus Christ did not write anything. It might be worth
your pondering the possible reasons for this. He left
behind him not a book, but a band of men and women who
were convinced of the truth of his resurrection and who
felt their lives to be changed by that event and to be
sustained by a new impetus which they called the Holy
Spirit. One of the salient facts about this young Church
was its sense of divine guidance.

The word which they used to describe this total
experience was *euangelion* – the Good News – a word used
by Jesus himself and taking up that used by Isaiah in
chapter 61, verse 1. It is usually translated 'Gospel'. This
Gospel was being transmitted by word of mouth long before
any Christian writings had appeared. But you cannot
distinguish between the authority of the Gospel and that of
the Church. They are one and the same thing. The Gospel
has no existence except as the authentic experience of the
Church. They are both equally *of God.*

The Church, and its Gospel, existed happily without a
New Testament throughout the period of its 'first, fine,
careless rapture.' When Christian writings began to appear
we know nothing of their status as authorities. But, as time
went on, other people began to produce variant versions of
'Christian' belief.

Most of these can be included in the term 'Gnostic'.
Basically they regarded the world as evil and could not,
therefore, attribute the Creation, let alone the Incarnation,
to God. They therefore rejected most of the Old Testament
and those Christian authors who made extensive use of it.

The Church had to make up its mind what writings it
did hold as being authoritative. We know very little about
the process. There seems to have been a general
consensus. But, if you ask why books such as 'the Book of
James' or 'the Gospel of Nicodemus' or 'the Gospel of Peter'
or 'the Epistle of Barnabas' are not included in the New
Testament, the answer is that the Church did not accept

them as representing sufficiently accurately the Gospel with
which it had been entrusted.

The authority of the Church guarantees the authority of
the New Testament as an authentic record of its Gospel.
How can that be 'sinister'?

AUTHORITY OF THE BIBLE

*'How far is biblical authority a matter of private, individual
response?'*

I LIKE Cranmer's phrase: 'in the Scriptures be the fat
pastures of the soul.' There is certainly something
individual about nourishment.

In the Middle Ages the Catholic Church believed the
Bible to have been written 'at the dictation of the Holy
Ghost.' Medieval miniatures depicting any one of the
evangelists often show the Dove perched on his shoulder
dictating while he writes. But the Church reserved to itself
the right of interpretation, and its method of interpretation
was largely based on a saying of Augustine's: 'whatever in
Holy Writ cannot be properly said to be concerned either
with morality or with faith must be recognized as
allegorical.' Thus the four rivers of Eden were 'explained'
as representing the cardinal virtues.

This allegorizing would strike most people today as
always arbitrary and often absurd, but the important point
to notice is that this method in effect transfers the
authority from the Scripture to the interpreter. It left the
final word with the Church – which meant, ultimately, with
the Pope. When the reformed Churches repudiated the
authority of the Papacy, they were left with the Bible and
the idea that it was divinely inspired.

In the Church of England, Richard Hooker was one of
the first to see that the question of interpretation must
precede that of authority. There is no point in saying that
something is authoritative if you cannot state what it
means. But to Hooker that correct interpretation was the
function of the human reason. 'That which by right
exposition buildeth up Christian faith, being misconstrued,
breedeth error; between true and false construction, reason
must show.'

There is a further principle of interpretation which I
find most clearly expressed by Hobbes. 'It is not the bare

words, but the scope of a writer that giveth the true light
by which any writing is to be interpreted; and they that
insist upon single texts, without considering the main
design, can derive nothing from them clearly; but rather,
by casting atoms of Scripture as dust before men's eyes,
make everything more obscure than it is.'

Once again, in relating a text to the 'main design' or
'scope' of the writer, the reader is exercising his own
judgement. To some this will seem to be throwing the Bible
to the individual, subjective, interpretation. But I would
suggest that there is a difference, as C.H. Dodd puts it,
between 'having your own opinion and submitting to the
truth as it comes to you.' Human reason has a higher
status than private opinion.

KNOWING THE BIBLE

*'In spite of new translations and new lectionaries the average
regular churchgoer seems to be lamentably ignorant of the
Bible.'*

I QUITE agree with you. I do not know how many times I
have been taken through the Bible with the lectionary, and
yet a passage can still strike me with the freshness of
something I have never heard or read before.

But you must remember that our lectionary derives from
an age when most people were illiterate. If they did not
hear the Bible read through to them in church they had no
other means of access to its contents. But today, when
illiteracy is the exception, we should set our sights higher.

The question of Philip to the Eunuch – 'Understandest
thou what thou readest?' – has not lost its relevance, and
the answer is still: 'How can I, except some man guide me?'

There is a striking word used in the account of the walk
to Emmaus: 'Did not our hearts burn within us while he
opened to us the Scriptures?' The word *opened* suggests
making people free of something previously inaccessible to
them. The Bible's own view of how it should be studied
suggests that it does not yield its treasures to the
superficial reader.

We must make a clear distinction between reading and
studying. We must learn to dig deeper.

The answer, I think, does not lie in this or that
translation of the Bible. If a mechanic says that he does

not understand the word *carburettor*, it is no use casting about for a more intelligible synonym. He needs to be taught what the thing is. Once he has understood that, he will understand the name normally applied to it.

Part of the solution to your problem is to be sought in a demand for more expository preaching. I am more often thanked for doing a Bible-study on one of the lessons in the pulpit than for anything else. But the time we can devote to such preaching is extremely limited, and there are many other legitimate topics to which a preacher must feel obliged to attend.

If Bible-study could only become a regular week-day activity of our congregations, we would need to put far fewer eggs into the basket marked 'lectionary'. If the lectionary were relieved of the intolerable burden of being the only provision for our knowledge of Scripture, it could be more imaginatively designed so that each reading enhanced the particular act of worship for which it was prescribed.

SCRIPTURAL TRUTH

'Scholars nowadays say you can believe hardly anything in the New Testament. Is this so?'

THIS IS to a certain extent a case where 'a little learning is a dangerous thing,' and we might be well advised to observe the precept of Alexander Pope: 'drink deep or taste not.'

I am reminded of a parish priest who preached a careful sermon on some of the results of form criticism (which to him emphatically did not invalidate the truths of scripture) and was distressed to overhear one of his simpler-minded parishioners complaining afterwards, 'Fancy the Vicar saying that the Bible was untrue.'

The careful and often complex arguments of the scholar do not lend themselves to the sort of over-simplification implied by this question; and I certainly doubt if many of the scholars themselves have come to the conclusion that 'you can hardly believe anything in the New Testament,' or would wish to be represented as having said so.

But the question pin-points an important issue. Christianity in its origins was the religion of simple and often uneducated people, and yet it has proved capable of

satisfying some of the highest intellects – a Thomas
Aquinas, an Albert Schweitzer or a William Temple.
Obviously it must be capable of appeal to both ends of the
intellectual scale if it is to be universal.

So two important points must be made. One is that you
do not have to be a scholar at all to derive great strength
and great inspiration from the Bible. It has spoken direct
to countless simple people throughout the ages and helped
them to lead good and Christian lives. But it is always
better to have a guide, and such guidance is admirably
provided by the Bible Reading Fellowship. The authors who
write for the BRF are men in touch with what the scholars
are saying.

But you have a duty to pursue the problems of truth as
far as your intellect can take you, and there are many
scholars who possess the art of making themselves
intelligible to those who do not share their intellectual
equipment. For people of moderate educational standard the
works, for instance, of Stephen Neill (*Seeing the Bible
whole* or *One Increasing Purpose*) or of Tom Baker (*What is
the New Testament?*) could be an eye-opener to the real and
vital truths which the New Testament contains.